More praise for *The Way of Wonder*

"Heavily quoted and annotated, this book by author Haas is a thorough and well-researched work that sincerely attempts not only to teach, but also to encourage others to 'stop and smell the roses'. ...he certainly provides plenty of food for thought." Denise M. Clark (*Denise's Pieces Book Reviews*)

"This book really impressed me. The author manages to juxtapose quotations from Jack Kerouac, Yoda, Winnie-the-Pooh, Lao Tzu, and God (via Neale Donald Walsh) in total support of his own train of thought. That takes intellect!...He has achieved his goal of creating an aura of awe, wonder, and mystery in the mundane activities of daily living. ...a most stimulating read." Alicia Karen Elkins (*Gotta Write Network Reviews*)

"*The Way of Wonder* inspires us to rediscover the mystery of ourselves. Jack Haas delivers a wonderful message with thorough research. There are quotations about the positiveness of 'wondering' from people who have traveled all walks of life. I would recommend "*The Way of Wonder*" to anyone searching for the answers to a 'wonder-full' life." Judine Slaughter (*Express Yourself Books*)

"Recommended book of the week." ofspirit.com

Thanks to Maggie McGhee for her exceptional editing talents.

Library of Canada Cataloguing in Publication data:

Haas, Jack, 1966-
  The Way of Wonder

    Includes bibliographical references.
    ISBN 0-9731007-0-2

1. Ontology 2. Wonder (Philosophy) 3. Spirituality
4. Mysticism I. Title.
B105.W65H32 2002   111.1 C2002-910610-9

Published by Iconoclast Press:
Suite 144
3495 Cambie St.
Vancouver, BC.
V5Z 4R3
Canada

admin@iconoclastpress.com
website: www.iconoclastpress.com

"Spend some time every day in awe, in total, complete awe. ...A few minutes a day in total awe will contribute to your spiritual awakening faster than any metaphysics course."
Wayne W. Dyer

To Patrick Côtē, and Benjamin Tucker, for shining their lights upon my path, and helping me on my way.

PROLOGUE

This is a book about wonder, about the great enigma of life, about ourselves, and about God. It is a book about the absurd, inexplicable, fantastic 'miracle of being' which we are, and of which we know almost nothing, though we claim to know so much.

This is a book about how we might realize the magic of existence again; how we might forget our false selves, remember our true selves, and live, and love, and play in the great mystery all around, and within us- the great mystery of existence, of life, of God.

This is a book about being, not doing; it is about how we become ourselves without struggling; how we walk free without escaping the prison, and how we fly without leaving the ground. It is a book about our return to innocence, to our own pristine heaven within- to humble unknowing, or wise ignorance, as it were- which comes about when we lose the encumbering mass of images we have, at our great expense, created and become ensconced within. In doing so we regain the liberating experience of absolute unknowing, and the profundity of indescribable awe.

There is a cornucopia of quotes in this work, the magnitude of which seemed essential to reveal the extent of diverse individuals who have, throughout history, attempted to express their personal exhilaration with *being*. I have sought to bring together a great many of these disparate voices and yet produce a singular song; a song which has been sung from time immemorial until the present, in many different languages, under many different guises, for many different reasons. In doing so I have drawn from an abundant variety of different sources: from poets and writers, past and present, Taoists, Christians, Buddhists, Hindus, Sufis, Jungian proponents, occultists, laymen, artists, mystics, madmen, and a host of other inimitable voices. Within such distinct perspectives there is yet a common thread running through the fabric of our multifarious existence; a thread that has been spoken of, or written about, in many unique ways. This thread is the apocalypse of absolute incomprehension- the benediction of wonder- where ignorance is reborn, innocence is returned, and beauty is awoken from its slumber in the false. Such is the outcome when the mind becomes unglued from its preconceptions, theories, and facts, and finally forgets all it has learned, thus coming to look upon existence as if for the very first time.

Life is an amazing implausibility; explain it, or explain it away, however we try, it remains thoroughly astounding; to imagine life through the eyes of someone who has never before experienced it, is to acknowledge that it is, in the most remarkable sense, absolutely unimaginable.

Hence there is no 'meaning' that I am attempting to relate in this book, for meaning itself is the cause of our predicament, of our false walls, of our heart's division.

I do not seek to fill the reader with knowledge, understanding, or interpretations (that I leave to the pundits, preachers, and pedagogues). I have no 'truth', no method, nor solution to offer. I want simply to wipe the slate clean, to bury the old way, so as to resurrect the new; to smash walls down, instead of building them up further; to widen the hole through which we may again grow and become whole.

I hope only to present the antithesis to thesis, the unsolution to life, and the re-mystification of all that seems profane, and so to move our consciousness onward. I envision no specific destination.

6

CONTENTS

PART I: OF HEAVEN, HELL, AND REDEMPTION

CHAPTER 1: Rapture

"There was something beyond clarity here- it was *magic*. ...it was *extraordinary*. And the reason...was because I was just ignorant enough to be susceptible to that which is lost in the fine meshes of order and clarity."

Henry Miller[1]

"The man was now rejoicing, as if not understanding were a kind of creation."

Clarice Lispector[2]

"We are doomed to perdition each time life does not reveal itself as a miracle, each time the moment no longer moans in a supernatural shudder."

E. M. Cioran[3]

"Unexpectedly, there was a flash of that unapproachable power and strength that was physically shattering. The body became frozen into immobility and one had to shut one's eyes not to go off into a faint. It was completely shattering and everything that was didn't seem to exist. ...It was something indescribably great whose height and depth are unknowable."

Jiddu Krishnamurti[4]

---

1 *The Hamlet Letters*, p46
2 *The Apple in the Dark*
3 *A Short History of Decay*, p33
4 *Notebooks*, July 1961

All is magnificent. All is marvelous. All is mysterious.

We live in a world of impossibility, implausibility, and awe. We look, we see, we wonder. We experience the sudden opening to the inexplicable vastness, the weirdness, the overwhelming profundity, the utter miracle and magic of life, of ourselves, and of all that *is*.

These are the numinous moments when the monumental impossibility and spaciousness of existence opens up before and within us, granting us the rare and spectacular interruptions of our day-to-day consciousness. Call it what you will: wonder, awe, *satori*, *samadhi*, newness of mind, ignorance, innocence, original mind, or childlike perception- it is the hallmark of a mind which has come to know the incomprehensible magnitude of all and everything, and from which the individual is 'opened up' and therefore reunited with the Great Mystery which is our birthright.

"Is there a pure feeling which fails to betray the mixture of grace and imbecility, a blissful admiration without an eclipse of the intelligence?"
E.M. Cioran[5]

'Wonder' is the open freedom of the pure mind- the first and last pillar upon which the castle of the Spirit is built. It is the beginning and the end, the home and the journey there.

Such rapture, then, is arguably the highest expression of our intimacy (or completeness) with the mystery of life. It is the point where the mind and heart merge in the overwhelming grace and splendor of Being. It is the shattering of all lesser realities, the divination of the profane, and the apotheosis of the damned.

---

5 *A Short History of Decay*, p156

It is the soul's remembrance of Paradise, the mind's remembrance of innocence, and the heart's remembrance of infinite love.

That is, we fall into wonder and begin to dwell in the inexhaustible state of creation's majesty, not when we try to build up understandings and perspectives, but, instead, when we become exhausted of all logic, reason, ideas, and profane perceptions.

In fact, we grasp onto static ideas, perspectives, and preconceptions about what life is to our own detriment. For, to not wonder, to not see the miracle of life at every moment, to not continually open ourselves, completely embracing the ever-present beauty and implausibility of all that is, is to exist within the prison of a limiting context.

"What is bad? What is good? What does one live for?
Who am I? What is life and What is death?"
Leo Tolstoy[6]

What is it to be? Why are we here? What are we? Who are you? Where shall we ground ourselves and find footing in the blessed, miracle of life? How could it be that we, who are life itself, can find life such a peculiar happening?

Rumi wrote:

"All day I think about it, then at night I say it.
Where did I come from, and what am I supposed to be doing?
I have no idea.
...who is it now in my ear, who hears my voice?
Who says words with my mouth?

---

6 *War and Peace*, p460

Who looks out with my eyes? What is the soul?
I cannot stop asking."[7]

And the crazy mystic, Osho, makes it quite obvious what
the real question is, as he relentlessly queries: "Who am I? Who
am I? Who am I? Who am I? Who am I? Who am I? Who am I?
Who am I? Who am I? Who am I? Who am I? Who am I? Who
am I? Who am I?"[8]

There now, everything has been condensed down to its
most purified essence; in a great, bewildering universe- the
dimensions, characteristics, and complexities of which cannot
help but create limitless inquiry for anyone who takes honest
account of such an unfathomable existence- there remains yet
one mystery which stands out above all else as the essential
conundrum: Who am I? What am I? Why am I? In short, what is
this 'I' that I am?

This 'question of questions' was addressed by Thomas
Carlyle, who stated: "With men of a speculative turn, there come
seasons, meditative, sweet, yet awful hours, when in wonder and
fear you ask yourself that unanswerable question: Who am *I*; The
thing that can say 'I'? ...[Your] sight reaches forth into the void
Deep, and you are alone with the Universe, and silently
commune with it, as one mysterious Presence with another.
...Who am I; what is ME? A voice, a Motion, an Appearance-
some embodied visualized Idea in the Eternal Mind? ...but
whence? How? Where to?"[9]

The mystery of self and the universe is astounding, the
questioning is limitless, yet what we are seeking is an answer-
that is all we want. And, in fact, there is an answer. But the
beautiful and tragic aspect of the response is that the answer is

---

7 *The Essential Rumi*
8 *Kundalini*, p51. Osho is also known as the Bhagwan Shree Rajneesh.
9 *Sartor Restorus*, p39

not really an answer at all- it is merely a recapitulation of the questions.

"I've told you time and again that the world is unfathomable. And so are we, and so is everything that exists in this world."
Don Juan to Carlos Castaneda[10]

There it is- our 'answer'; an answer which has not solved the questions, but has instead merely magnified them.

Life is an unknowable, inexplicable miracle; there is no solution, and ...there is not supposed to be a solution. It is all an unsolvable mystery, and is unreachably far beyond the mind's ken. And that includes the self, like it or not.

In fact, "Truth is known in such a way", declared Osho, "that by knowing it the mystery does not disappear; in fact it becomes very, very deep, infinitely deep, ultimately deep. By knowing the truth, nothing is solved. In fact for the first time you are facing the insoluble. This is the paradox, the dilemma!"[11]

Now, have we solved anything with such simple, circular logic? No, we have solved nothing. And yet ...that is the solution- a solution which was described by William James as such: "Existence then will be a brute fact to which as a whole the emotion of ontological wonder shall rightfully cleave, but remain eternally unsatisfied. Then wonderfulness or mysteriousness will be an essential attribute of the nature of things, and the

---

10 *Tales of Power*, p45
11 *Ecstasy: The Language of Existence*, p126. Similarly, M. Scott Peck stated: "The understanding of basic reality is never something we achieve; it is only something that can be approached. And, in fact, the closer we approach it the more we realize we do not understand- The more we stand in awe of its mystery." (*People of the Lie*, p42). Summarizing this observation, Dante conceded: "This is all some sort of miracle, fresh, amazing."

exhibition and emphasizing of it will continue to be an ingredient in the philosophic industry of the race."[12]

That is, to fully accept the ontological ramifications of this epistemological realization- that life is an inexplicable enigma, that everything we have called knowledge is false, that everything we have thought we are is wrong, that nothing is what we think it is, and that the entirety of life is impressively implausible- is to have come to the state of innocent wondering, of rapture.

> *"Understanding is not a piercing of the mystery, but an*
> *acceptance of it, a living blissfully with it,*
> *in it, through and by it."*
> Henry Miller[13]

'Wonder', then, is the moment when the answerless questions of the universe become not only fully obvious, but electrifying; it is the point where the individual is released from the limiting possibility that life is knowable, and the mind is cut free from the cognitive fetters which enclose it.

To embrace the feeling of exasperation, of incomprehension- to enter into the feeling of rapture, which is the mind's purest state- is to ground ourselves nowhere, find no footing, and forget everything we have ever been told, and so to return to the sense of intoxicating awe. We must, as it is said- become as children. And that means to look without labels, knowledge, or expectation, and instead to see and be new at every moment; to forget what we think life is, and to allow ourselves not to know what it is- that is exaltation.

---

12 *Will to Believe*, p72
13 *The Wisdom of the Heart*

Sam Keen describes the experience as such: "Wonder begins with the element of surprise. The now almost obsolete word 'wonderstruck' suggests that wonder breaks into consciousness with a dramatic suddenness that produces amazement or astonishment. ...Because of the suddenness with which it appears, wonder reduces us momentarily to silence. We associate gaping, breathlessness, bewilderment, and even stupor with wonder, because it jolts us out of the world of common sense in which our language is at home. The language and categories we customarily use to deal with experience are inadequate to the encounter, and hence we are initially immobilized and dumbfounded. We are silent before some new dimension of meaning which is being revealed."[14]

It is this essential recognition- accepting that all life is inconceivable- that would cause Nikos Kazantzakis, in his book, *The Last Temptation of Christ,* to have Jesus, after being requested to perform a miracle, disdainfully proclaim, "Everything is a miracle... What further miracles do you want? Look below you: even the humblest blade of grass has its guardian angel who stands by and helps it grow. Look above you: what a miracle is the star-filled sky! And if you close your eyes...what a miracle the world within us!"[15]

What a miracle life is indeed.

"All is doubtful, all is mysterious, all is intoxicating."
Aleister Crowley[16]

It is this vision of 'wonder'- a vision which looks with

---

14 *Apology for Wonder*, p28
15 *The Last Temptation of Christ,* p301
16 *The Book of Thoth*, p113

no facts, myths, theories, or words to ground us, and decontextualizes the entire event of being- that allows us to see life as magical and new, over and over again, so that there is no end to novelty and awe. [17]

Osho claimed, "...the absurd is the beautiful and the beautiful is always absurd. ...Each moment is so precious, and each moment brings such precious rewards, you just enjoy it. Get lost in it. Be drunk with life..."[18]

> *"The most beautiful thing we can experience*
> *is the mysterious."*
> Albert Einstein

Beauty and mystery are seen when we have the tenacity to look at the world without the hindrance of anything we have ever been told, nor of anything we believe we know, for isn't a flower more beautiful without the word flower containing it? Is it not, in fact, our truest nature to look so deeply into the heart of things that the words we hide them behind vaporize from our minds and we are left with naught but the naked miracle in everything we see, and everything we do?

Henry Miller expounded upon this doctrine when he wrote: "The task of genius, and man is nothing if not genius, is to keep the miracle alive, to live always in the miracle, to make the miracle more and more miraculous, to swear allegiance to nothing, but live only miraculously, think only miraculously, die miraculously."[19]

---

17 "Life is so strange! It is nothing I have ever been able to take for granted, just simply being alive with the world in front of my eyes and looking out through those eyes at the world", wrote Russell Hoban (*Pilgermann*, p69).
18 *Ecstasy*, p130
19 *The Colossus of Marousi*, p88

To live in the moment always conscious of the mystery of existence, of the fact that whatever this life is, it is a momentous imponderability, and that we also are this same incredible profundity, is to accept this sense of marvel as the essence of our very core.

> *"If you study life deeply, its profundity will seize you suddenly with dizziness."*
> Albert Schweitzer

The rapture of wonderment is its own reward, its own validation, its own argument against all else, for the authenticity of absolute ignorance washes the world so unimaginably clean, that no logic, nor polemic, nor art can ever again match, dispel, or compete with the reality of such a moving occurrence.

Swami Premgeet declared: "Life is full of wonder. We taste it in our childhood, lose it as we grow up, and if we are lucky catch the magic again in those precious moments which make life a joy. The echo may return in the eyes of a beloved, in the first burst of morning light, or in a thousand unexpected forms. When it comes we are suddenly in the presence of the miraculous, we are taken by that elusive sense of being part of a great whole. These are the moments when our energy expands to encompass something beyond ourselves."[20]

Similarly, Walt Whitman poetically wrote:

"I believe a leaf of grass is not less than the journey-
work of the stars,
And the pismire is equally perfect, and a grain
of sand, and the egg of the wren,

---

20 Introduction to *Kundalini*, by Osho

16

And the tree-toad is a chef-d'oeuvre for the highest,
And the running blackberry would adorn the
parlors of heaven,
And the narrowest hinge in my hands puts to scorn
all machinery,
And the cow crunching with depress'd head
surpasses any statue,
And a mouse is miracle enough to stagger sextillions
of infidels."[21]

This last passage is reminiscent of the enviable vision of a child or a fool, sitting on the ground in rapt attention at the simplest things which we pass by every day obliviously because our minds have gotten in the way and have thus made the miracle of life a commonplace event.

Dropping everything out of the mind leads us back to infinity, for the vision of wonder is not limited. We must simply have no walls of fear or interpretation, and dismiss our useless cares, so as to stop, to breathe, to smile, to exalt.

"That mystic baffling wonder alone completes all."
Walt Whitman

And how does the exaltation of wonder 'complete all'? Carl Jung explains: "It is important to have a secret, a premonition of things unknown. It fills life with something impersonal, a *numinosum*. A man who has never experienced that has missed something important. He must sense that he lives in a world which in some respects is mysterious; that things happen and can be experienced which remain inexplicable; that

---

21 *Song of Myself,* from *Leaves of Grass*

17

not everything which happens can be anticipated. The unexpected and the incredible belong in this world. Only then is life whole. For me the world has from the beginning been infinite and ungraspable."[22]

This is the world in which we truly live, if only we would leave the land of exile- the exile called 'knowing'- and take up conscious residence in bliss and rapture within the Great Mystery itself.

"The sense of wonder, that is our sixth sense.
And it is the natural religious sense."
D.H. Lawrence

Of this sense, the Reverend John Claypool sermonized rhapsodically: "...ecstasy- the experience of 'rising up with wings as eagles.' Here is an utterly authentic way for the life of God to come into our lives, and the experience of such moments of exuberance and abandon and celebration has always been a part of biblical religion. There is a hint from the very beginning that this is part of the nature of God himself. Do you recall how one of the Genesis accounts depicts God as looking out over all he had been creating and finding it 'very good'? He promptly proceeded to take a day off simply to celebrate the wonder of 'isness'. This is ecstasy. ...[And so] to lose one's self in wonder, awe, and praise, to forget one's self before the mystery of God- I would have defined that as the highest spiritual achievement."[23]

---

22 *Memories, Dreams, Reflections.* p356
23 *The Light Within You*, p135, 214. Similarly Joseph Campbell states: "...that, exactly, is the way it has always appeared to those in whom wonder- and not salvation- is religion." (*Oriental Mythology*, p36) And the converted singer Van Morrison seems to have come to this same realization, as he crooned: "I'm a soul in wonder...I'm a soul in wonder...I'm a soul in wonder..."

The way in which wonder and mystery have been the cornerstones of many different spiritual and secular paths will be exposed as we move through the following chapters. The important thing, however, is not to have notions about rapture, but to experience rapture itself.

As such, the incredibly idiosyncratic, iconoclastic, and obscure Tibetan Buddhist text, the *kun byed rgyal po'i mdo* (or, The Sovereign All-Creating Mind, The Motherly Buddha), states: "It is worthwhile to rejoice in the way the sentient beings appear as to their form, appearance, and color. ...One rejoices in them due to a method of not-at-all thinking. ...[Then] whatever comes into existence is My wonder. ...This miraculous and wonderful joy rests like the sky in the deedless. ...If you do not perceive 'That' as being different from ignorance, instantly, That comes forth by itself. ...I tell you, do not try to intellectualize this! I recommend that you, oh great bodhisattva, will teach the hosts of retinues in the same way as I taught you."[24]

Let us go now, down the forgotten labyrinths of our infinite selves, where, at every turn, if we are open, and honest, and innocent enough we shall discover more mystery, madness, miracle, and magic. Limitations are of the mind. Incomprehénsion is our freedom. Let us go.

"We would give you vast and strange domains," offers Guillaume Apollinaire, "Where flowering mystery waits for him who would pluck it."

*****

---

24 pl 12,64,76

CHAPTER 2: The Myth of Knowing

"You beg me to come closer to the heart of our subject. What is our subject if not the grievous effect of knowledge."
    Henry Miller[1]

"There had been a wearing away of his previous knowledge, and as far as words, he only knew them as a person who had once suffered from them- as if he had been cured."
    Clarice Lispector[2]

"History is nothing but a procession of false Absolutes, a series of temples raised to pretexts, a degradation of the mind before the Improbable."
    E.M. Cioran[3]

"...to see...with eyes that have been bathed in emptiness, that have not been hurt with knowledge- to see then is an extraordinary experience."
    Jiddu Krishnamurti[4]

1 *The Hamlet Letters*
2 *The Apple in the Dark*, p109
3 *A Short History of Decay*, p3
4 *Freedom from the Known*

We have seen the light, now it is time for us to walk through the darkness. Let us see exactly why it is that life, for most of us, feels less like the living miracle which it is, and more like a troubling complex of inharmonious occurrences.

What happens is that though life begins for most children as a bewildering entry into a magical, mythical, incredible world, the great majority of us get pushed out of the wonders of childhood without ever knowing what has happened; we get 'schooled' and mentally trapped early, get caught in pre-fabricated, obtusely delineated lives, and never again awaken to the wonder of our own existences and of this mysterious creation. Instead we spend our days confined in futile acts of triviality which only succeed in hemming us in further. We get lost in a labyrinth of facts, ideas, preconceptions, and societal 'truths', and in doing so we forget the fact that life is not a simple event which is easily contained in the boxes the mind requires in order to function within humanity's prefigured conditions; we forget the miracle, the mystery, and the confounding implausibility of all and everything, including ourselves. And that is a great tragedy.

> *"Rabbit's clever," said Pooh thoughtfully.*
> *"Yes," said Piglet, "Rabbit's clever."*
> *"And he has Brain."*
> *"Yes," said Piglet, "Rabbit has Brain."* ...
> *"I suppose," said Pooh,*
> *"that that's why he never understands anything."*
> Winnie-the-Pooh[5]

There are many lies which hide themselves from us

---

5 *Winnie-the-Pooh* by A.A. Milne

under the guise of assertions, assumptions, and appearances, but really they are all products of the first lie- The Lie, The Big Lie- and that lie is ...that we understand.

The indoctrination into the dogma of false certitude begins at birth, accelerates exponentially through the ubiquitous incarceration called school, and is fertilized and fostered by every institution we encounter throughout our lives, from the church, to the media, the marketers, and the family. Rarely is the innocent mind cultivated.

This cognitive corruption is committed unwittingly by nearly every society on earth; from our earliest years we are confined to mental boxes, are force-fed a massive amount of useless information, and then punished if we fail to regurgitate the 'truths' as they are told to us. Most of us, in essence, have been brainwashed by learning.

"Men are born ignorant, not stupid;
they are made stupid by education."
Bertrand Russell

And J. Krishnamurti stated: "Living in such a corrupt, stupid society as we do...the competitive education we receive...warps, twists, and dulls our days."[6]

That is, we are greatly blinded by institutional learning, because we are stuffed to fullness with an indigestible banquet of unreal, or unnecessary, words, facts, and theorems.

One of E.M. Cioran's caustic volleys against such useless learning runs as follows: "How imagine other people's lives, when our own seems scarcely conceivable? We meet someone, we see him plunged into an impenetrable and

---

6 *Freedom from the Known*, p41

unjustifiable world, in a mass of desires and convictions superimposed on reality like a morbid structure. Having made a system of mistakes for himself, he suffers for reasons whose nullity alarms the mind and surrenders himself to values whose absurdity leaps to the eye. What are his undertakings but trifles, and is the feverish symmetry of his concerns any better built than an architecture of twaddle?"[7]

That is, by learning falsely, we invent false problems, and seek false solutions, then we live falsely, and teach falsity. It is a vicious circle which has no end.

"From the day we went to school we learned nothing;
on the contrary, we were made obtuse,
we were wrapped in a fog of words and abstractions."
Henry Miller[8]

Recognizing this, Grace Llewellyn- in her tragically little-known book *The Teenage Liberation Handbook*, which is designed to assist youths in escaping from their pedantic tormentors- quotes an eighth-grade student, who says, "The average second grader is a person slightly smarter than the average third grader, because they've had a year less of school."[9]

This is an absurd statement, and yet it is only absurd to an absurd society that defends its false reality by the tactical method of teaching its delusions to each younger generation, thus perpetuating the mental ossification.[10]

---

7 *A Short History of Decay*, p18
8 *Tropic of Capricorn*, p129
9 *The Teenage Liberation Handbook*, p28
10 This indeed is the case, as Sigmund Freud pessimistically noted: "What a distressing contrast there is between the radiant intelligence of the child and the feeble mentality of the average adult." And Christopher Hyatt admitted: "I felt that I was getting more stupid

Yes indeed, how truly barbaric it is that during the essential years of curiosity and wonder- when it would be much healthier for our bodies and souls to be outside amongst the wind and the trees, singing, and dancing, and playing about- we are instead corralled foolishly into a holding tank, and there we are injected continually with the bitter medicine of dubious realities.

"So far as concepts are concerned, they are all lies."
Swamiji Shyam[11]

We see now that many different individuals have come to the uncomfortable realization that what we have called learning is not learning at all, and what we have thought was truth is not true all, and what we were told was useful knowledge was nothing more than 'twaddle'.

The ever recalcitrant, Thomas Carlyle, had even less glowing words for his mentors; in his aggressively rhetorical style, he avowed: "My teachers were hide-bound Pedants, without knowledge of man's nature, or of boy's; or of aught save their lexicons and quarterly account books. Innumerable dead Vocables...they crammed into us, and called it fostering the growth of mind. How can an inanimate, mechanical Gerund-grinder, the like of whom will, in a subsequent century, be manufactured at Nurunberg out of wood and leather, foster the growth of anything, much more of the mind, which grows not like a vegetable...but like a spirit, by mysterious contact of Spirit. ...[A true] man deals much in the feeling of Wonder; insists on the necessity and high worth of universal Wonder; which he

---

as I was getting older. This, as I was to find out later, was a result of higher education."
(*Rebels and Devils*, p20)
11 Talks, 2000

24

holds to be the only reasonable tempter for the denizen of so singular a Planet as ours. Wonder...is the basis of Worship; The reign of wonder is perennial, indestructible in Man. ...[And] science, which is to destroy Wonder, and in its stead substitute Mensuration and Numeration, finds small favour [with us]... Above all, that class of Logic-choppers, and trebble-pipe Scoffers, and professed Enemies of Wonder; who, in these days, so numerously patrol as night-constables about the Mechanic's Institute of Science, and cackle, like true Old-Roman geese and goslings round their Capitol, on any alarm, or on none; nay, who often, as illumined Sceptics, walk abroad into peaceable society, in full day-light, with rattle and lantern, and insist on guiding you and guarding you therewith, though the Sun is shining... That whole class is inexpressibly wearisome. ...[For] the man who cannot wonder, who does not habitually wonder...is but a Pair of Spectacles behind which there is no Eye."[12]

Put bluntly (as if it has not been put bluntly enough already): knowledge is dishonesty. Our teachers could only make excuses for not understanding anything, and these excuses were what they call 'knowing'. And then, from this first, gigantic error,

---

12 *Sartor Restorus*, p 80,50. Carlyle then directed his luminous fire at such a person as he has just described in the last sentence, admonishing: "Thou wilt have no Mystery and Mysticism; wilt walk through the world by the sunshine of what thou callest Truth, or even by the hand-lamp of what I call Attorney-Logic; and 'explain' all, 'account' for all, or believe nothing? Nay, thou wilt attempt laughter; [but] whoso recognizes the unfathomable, all-pervading domain of Mystery, which is everywhere under our feet and among our hands; to whom the Universe is an Oracle and Temple, as well as a Kitchen and Cattle stall- he shall be a delirious mystic; to him thou, with sniffing charity, will protrusively proffer thy hand lamp, and shriek, as one injured, when he kicks his foot through it... [You,] retire into private places with thy foolish cackle; or, what were better, give it up, and weep, not that the reign of wonder is done...but that thou hitherto art a Dilettante and sandblind Pedant." (p52) As with Carlyle, the rebel bohemian, Jack Kerouac, in his invective, poetic-prose contends: "...colleges [are] nothing but grooming schools for the middle-class non-identity... while [others] ...go prowling in the wilderness to hear the voice crying in the wilderness, to find the ecstasy of the stars, to find the dark mysterious secret of the origin of faceless wonderless crapulous civilization." *Dharma Bums*, p35

25

there erupted the dogma of learning their 'truths', which then continued the irrevocable chain of indoctrination so perniciously administered under the false auspices of 'learning'. But such learning is a shackle on the freedom of the soul, a cage built around a fledgling bird.[13]

> *"...your ideas are false, for all ideas are false."*
> Sri Nisargadatta Maharaj[14]

It is obvious now that to continue stumbling onward in the same infantile direction as our teachers, leaders, and ancestors is to continue bashing our heads against the same walls, and to have not yet learned the one thing made obvious from all our learning- that ...learning is useless.

False education is what restricts the mystery, inducing facts. True education is what expands the mystery, educing wonder. But the sad case is that education today rarely educes, and mostly induces; it induces inertia, confusion, stagnation, and futility.[15]

---

13 The *kun byed rgyal po'i mdo* states: "Oh, the sentient beings...are of coarse intelligence. Due to their nature which draws their senses towards objects, these ignorant beings are content with whatever they are taught."(p176) And Ramtha corroborates this position contending: "...we've only been taught what we aren't, not what we are. ...For man, the timid seeker of truth, wishing so desperately to be accepted, will listen to any folly. ...the atrocity of [thus] being closed-minded is that it keeps you from knowing joy. It keeps you from knowing the glory of yourself and God. As long as you have a cloistered mind and live and think according to social consciousness, you will never venture into the unknown, or contemplate the possibility of greater realities..." (*Destination Freedom II*, p146,180)

14 *I AM THAT*, p105

15 David Icke states: "Education seems to be a wonderful thing. I agree, so it's about time we had some. We do not have education today, we have indoctrination. The teachers have become teachers by telling the system what it wants to hear because that is the only way they pass their exams. If they don't absorb the system's version of life, they don't become teachers and lecturers. Then they must tell this same story to the students of the

It is our lot to have inherited the lie which our forefathers were neither lucid enough to see, nor strong enough to break away from. We must now simply have the strength and honesty to see 'what is' as it is, without the imposition of words, labels, judgements, or theories. We must no longer seek for explanations of the unexplainable, for to 'explain', is to explain away the mystery. [16]

To become undulled from our past 'education', all we need to do is to wake up to the lie of 'understanding', and let life return of its own accord, as it is so inherently wont to do, to its implausible, grandiose, marvelous stature. [17]

E.M. Cioran observes: "...all of life's evils come from a 'conception of life', [for] under each formula lies a corpse..." [18]

Any restriction, any limitation, rule, or order placed upon life, and wonder is gone.

Life with beauty of mystery, then, requires the courage to dis-believe, the strength to not-understand, the fortitude to renounce everything the world believes to be true, and so to stand naked and alone, without a single thought to hold onto.

"If man is to survive, he must never cease wondering."
Sam Keen[19]

---

next generation. Otherwise they won't stay professors and teachers. Their students write all this stuff down, and if they don't tell their exam paper what the system wants to hear they don't pass their exams. It is a self-perpetuating cycle. ...Once you have conditioned one generation to [a] narrow version of reality, they will, as parents and teachers, indoctrinate the next generation to believe the same thing. So it gets passed on across generations." (*Lifting the Veil*, p130)

16 As the parsimonious master Dzogchen relates, "There is no concept that can define the condition of 'what is'."

17 Swamiji Shyam asserts: "You have to be free from all your concepts. Where you cannot make a concept, that is freedom." (Talks, March 1999)

18 *A Short History of Decay*, p5,7

19 *Apology for Wonder*, p17

27

One of the hindrances to absolute wonder is the vanity of mind which believes it can understand what is far beyond its capability.[20] And so, the world of 'learning' is dangerous because from it we learn largely to know life improperly, and the mind would rather know improperly than not at all.

The blame lies not just on academia, but on the whole infrastructure of particularization and mentalization. Luckily, however, though learning may blind us it cannot destroy the mystery of being. As H. L. Mencken optimistically pointed out: "Penetrating so many secrets, we cease to believe in the unknowable. But there it sits nonetheless, calmly licking its chops."

It is merely our task to open our eyes again, without any lens between life and ourselves.

As such we must renounce scholarship for exactly the very same reason that it is justified: that is, we must renounce it because through academia and book-learning people are taught to believe that they 'understand' things. And yet all this 'understanding' does is allow us to misunderstand and misuse our marvelous selves, thus denying us our rightful place in a world of wonder.

Byron lamented: "Sorrow is knowledge: they who know the most/ must mourn the deepest o'er the fatal truth,/ the tree of knowledge is not that of life."[21]

None of us are free of sorrow, and none of us are innocent, for we have all 'gone to bed with the devil' so to

---

20 Stepan Stulginsky declared: "We've grown very proud and forgot about everything unknown to us." (*Cosmic Legends of the East*, p129)

21 *Manfred*, lines 10-12, act1, sc1. The Tree of Knowledge and the concomitant misery of the eating of its fruit will be expanded more deeply upon in the chapter on 'The Fall'. For now it is perhaps enough to say that the cognitive aspect of the 'Fall', spoken of in the Old Testament, should be obvious to the sensitive reader, simply by re-cognizing the assertion of that bold and chilling line from Ecclesiastes- "For in much wisdom is much grief: and he that increaseth knowledge increaseth sorrow." (1:18)

speak.

The equation is simple: knowledge equals sorrow. And why is that? Easy enough: because existence is unknowable, and therefore to 'know' it is to not know it; that is, to believe that we understand what cannot be understood, is to disfigure it, and therefore to exist in a unreal way, which equals sorrow. 'Unknowability' is the essence, the inherent, underlying reality of everything. And so, the more we separate ourselves from what we inherently are- mystery- the more we 'fall' away from our highest possibility.

"Deplorable mania, when something happens, to inquire what?
Can it be I am the prey of a genuine preoccupation,
of a need to know as one might say?"
Samuel Becket[22]

I am not here suggesting that we revert to a world community of idle idiots; it is not that we must give up the mind, as such, but only the assumption of 'understanding' what we are, what life is, and how we must therefore live it. For true living asks only one thing of us- to live. And we cannot do this in the boxes of mind; neither in the physical, nor in the metaphysical worlds.

"To be full of knowledge breeds endless misery", admitted J. Krishnamurti.[23]

Facts, words, truths, and propositions: these are the interruptions of the soul's joy at its own miraculousness, because no explanation of this event, of 'what is', no matter how profound or valid, can possibly do justice to the

22 *The Unnameable*, p294
23 *Journal*, Sept 1973

overwhelmingness of life's occurrence.

'Idea' *is* negligence. Understanding is an entombment- a sepulcher of certitude. 'Knowing' buries the knower who ends up not filled with the living spirit, but, instead, embalmed with lifeless understandings. And it is these little understandings which we accumulate that simply prevent us from attaining the Great Non-understanding. 'Knowledge' is a stranglehold we are taught to place upon ourselves; by trying to know the unknowable we simply suffocate the true breath of mystery out of life.

"Ghosts wailed at night when the ancients invented word", decried the Chinese poet Kung Tzu-chen, "A hundred anxieties beset men of later ages who know how to read."[24]

Knowledge settles heavily upon us, like an oppressive weight built of things and meanings; we say "I understand", and we die ignorant within that knowing. And the reason for this is that it is not really 'knowing'.

"Conventional knowledge", declared Rumi, "is a death to our souls, and it is not really *ours*." And his spiritual brother, Kabir, who never valued reading, writing, words, or learning, affirmed: "With the word 'reason' you already feel miles away."

Yes indeed, and not only the word 'reason', but also logic, truth, correctness, understanding- the whole lot of these words can be dismissed as failures.

> *"...life is tolerable only by the degree*
> *of mystification we endow it with."*
> E.M. Cioran [25]

24 from *Sunflower Splendor*
25 *A Short History of Decay*, p105

Which is to say, knowledge is alien to our incomprehensible beings, and so, by envisioning ourselves through thought's limited lenses, we become aliens to ourselves.

"['Knowing']...is an evasion of the courage to be; it prevents the absorption of maximum meaninglessness into oneself", stated Ernest Becker in his Pulitzer Prize winning book, *The Denial of Death*.[26] Becker's thesis is that the greater part of mankind's woes and sorrows arise from an inability to accept mortality, and so, via various escapes and repressions, he says, we end up living lives of complete fantasy, denial, and absurdity. I would assert, however, that our ills arise not from a denial of death, but ...from a denial of life! For what is life but mystery? So to deny mystery is to deny life.

Yet we are so brutally corrupted by a relentless assault of unquestioned, deviously articulate, mediocre nonsense, that it is almost impossible to purge the rot which thickly binds us. 'Truth', as we learn it, is epistemological suicide.

"To turn that magnificence out there into reasonableness doesn't do anything for you. Here, surrounding us, is eternity itself. To engage in reducing it to a manageable nonsense is petty and outright disastrous."
Don Juan[27]

We were not intended to fall into the mundane inertia of

---

26 *The Denial of Death*, p280
27 *Tales of Power*, by Carlos Castaneda, p31. Similarly, Sam Keen observed: "By understanding the positive relationship between mystery and knowledge we see the fallacy of the romantic notion that an increase of knowledge leads to an eclipse of wonder. Knowledge destroys mystery and wonder ...when it is used hostilely to reduce the dimensions of meaning in an object to those that can be manipulated and controlled." (*Apology for Wonder*, p26)

our wonderless society, and live our whole lives through, seeing only from the limited vantage points provided by the world of the word. We were not intended to live enveloped by fragile misinterpretations- to cling to the veneer of 'meaning'; we were intended to release these and apprehend unmeaning. We were intended to witness limitlessness, in ourselves, our fellows, and everything we come upon.

Cioran observed: "In the Mind's graveyard lie the principles and the formulas: the Beautiful is defined, and interred there. And like it the True, the Good, knowledge, and the Gods- they are all rotting there. ...Consider the accent with which a man utters the word 'truth', the inflection of assurance or reserve he uses, the expression of believing or doubting it, and you will be edified as to the nature of his opinions and the quality of his mind. No word is emptier..."[28]

"What kills life, is the absence of mystery."
Anais Nin[29]

The libertarian and friend of Anais Nin, Henry Miller, was equally nauseated by the conventional process of thought. He declared: "This is a mania- *explaining* things. It goes with a certain type of mind which I abhor. And always leaves me with the feeling that nothing is explained, that we are simply eating into a hole. ...The good thinkers are a race apart and they leave a bad smell behind them. You think perhaps they penetrated a little further into the unknown than the ordinary fellow? That is a great falsehood. The unknown is a constant and the advances we make into it are illusory. I love the unknown precisely because it

---

28 *A Short History of Decay*, p119, 167
29 *Anais Nin's Diaries*

is a 'beyond', because it *is* impenetrable."[30]

That is, the mind cannot elucidate the mystery of the universe to us, it can only falsely convince us; it convinces us that we comprehend the incomprehensible. And this false certitude, that we then carry through life as our guide, is far from the open acceptance of honest ignorance which would bring to us the reality of our marvelous existence.

Life is so far beyond us that the statement "I understand" is a person's first lie to themselves; certainty is like a psychopathological condition; the confidence of facts and theorems is a mangling lobotomy; by 'explanation' we condemn ourselves to the explainable. The least of concepts mutilates the innocent mind.

We are best to ease back into the gentle splendor of puzzlement, regarding the world with humble admiration, rather than invent understandings and then proceed to sheepishly convince ourselves that these are 'true'.

"Scientists are buffoons," claims Alan Lightman, "not because they are rational but because the cosmos is irrational."[31]

"There are more things in heaven and earth, Horatio, than are dreamt of in your philosophy."
William Shakespeare[32]

Indeed there are more incredible things than the mind can conclude.

Once certainty exists- once an individual believes either

---

30 *The Hamlet Letters*, p114,101
31 *Einstein's Dreams*, p41
32 *Hamlet.* "To them, [the men of the world]", concluded Aleister Crowley, "knowledge will be everything, and what is knowledge but the very soul of illusion?" (*Collected Works, Vol.1*, p111)

that they understand correctly, or that correct understanding is at least possible- 'interpretation' then becomes the tragic common ground between the sacred and the profane, between the mean and the miracle, between the unknown ...and the assumption of knowing. Which is to say, 'interpretation', or 'theory', as it were, defiles the magnitude of the mystery by making us think it is 'knowable'. Therefore, to grant this amazing life its true miraculousness is merely a matter of modestly admitting that we are not capable of knowing what life is all about- that it is beyond us ...way beyond us.

Knowledge leads not only away from wonder, but also towards worry; through the false particularization of life, suddenly there is a false matrix imposed upon the insouciant, singular play of being, and we find ourselves drowning within the confines of overbearing triviality. Life itself is not the problem; life does not impose cares upon the mind, the mind imposes cares upon life.

As such, our 'knowledge' generally falls into one of two categories: useless, or detrimental; either we don't need it, or we are thoroughly better without it.

One maverick who saw clearly the tragedy of false learning was Bob Marley, legendary for his lyrics, his revelry, and his passion for life ...for life's sake. In his words we find his love, and in his love we find his anger:

"Don't let them fool ya, or even try to school ya.
We've got a mind of our own, oh yeah!
Don't let them change ya, or even rearrange ya,
oh no!"

And:

"Emancipate yourself from mental slavery,

34

none but ourselves can free our minds."[33]

The teachings we have been 'given' (or, more precisely, have had foisted upon us) have carved the beautiful Garden into a horrid labyrinth of lostness. Adults adulterate the joyful givenness of life into an encumbering, burdenful yoke- a yoke which must be cast off, if we are to ever reach greener pastures.[34]

"Exterminate learning and there will no longer be worries."
Lao Tzu

The pursuit of facts is purely a fainthearted way to live upon this earth; 'thought' is a form of immature trembling, and 'knowledge' is simply our current catharsis for not being able to understand what is not understandable.
"Truth?", demanded Henri Barbusse, "What do they mean by it?"[35]
Ah yes, what do they 'mean'? What does 'meaning' actually mean? When we truly look into this word, we find that

---

33 From Pink Floyd's lyrics, a similar note of warning occurs; they sing: "We don't need no education, we don't need no thought control. ...[For] all in all it's just another brick in the Wall." And lyrics from the rock band Rush run: "Let's set aside the education, and get on with the fascination."
34 Sam Keen proffers: "Unlike some varieties of bees who come into the world to find that the previous generation has disappeared and left them only a store of food, human infants are raised by parents. And parents very often have ceased to wonder. Parents who are anxious about novelty communicate this attitude to their children: the world is to be suspected of being guilty and hostile until it proves itself otherwise. Needless to say, when a child adopts this attitude, the world seldom has a chance to prove its innocence. ...The underlying reason for the eclipse of wonder must be sought in the basic attitudes toward life and the fundamental models of man adopted by those who educate wonder out of children. The explanation for the loss does not lie in a genetic approach to the experience of children, but will be found, in the study of the pathology of adult experience." (*Apology for Wonder*, p58-59)
35 *The Inferno*, p9

35

the root of 'meaning' is 'mean' (this is a crucially important point in order to recognize one of our culture's more specious self-deceptions); the word 'meaning', which we have adopted as if synonymous with 'purpose', or 'the definition of', and which we have proceeded to use as a noun (i.e. 'to have meaning', or 'to find meaning'), is, instead, actually a verb which 'means' (if I may employ that misnomer now): 'to make mean'. And what is it to make 'mean'? It is to make something vulgar, prosaic, or mediocre- that is what we really get out of meaning. Meaning is meanness.[36]

> *"To seek for meaning is to cut open the ball*
> *in search of its bounce."*
> Roger Lancelyn Green[37]

Knowledge is a poor consolation, a worshipped failure, for it has not succeeded in emancipating us.

To explain a phenomenon is to distort it; knowledge is an epistemological catastrophe, for when we invest meaning into something that does not possess it inherently, we corrupt it to our own purposes. Which is to say- we 'know' it improperly, rather than unknowing it properly. But when finally we come to the necessary acceptance that we do 'not-know' we then merge easily into, and belong intimately with, the greater part of life, for that is when we no longer simply 'know' a fragment of the

---

36 A supporting, pithy diatribe, from the ever-truculent U.G. Krishnamurti, namesake of, but not to be confused with, Jiddu Krishnamurti, runs: "Don't look for a meaning to life; there may not be any meaning at all. It may have its own meaning that you can never know. ...That is all. You needn't impose a meaning upon it. ...You must face the fact that you know nothing about life or the living of it. ...All I am trying to point out to you is that all this knowledge you are so proud of flaunting isn't worth a tinker's damn." (*Mind is a Myth*, p102,121)
37 *Letters*, p388

whole, but instead we 'unknow' *all* of it. And since we have bound ourselves with ideas and theories, stunting the evolution of the untethered mind, we must now molt conceptually, or we shall remain dwarfed by the cramping encumbrance of outgrown meanings.

"Knowledge is not intelligence", admonished Herakleitos. And LaoTzu stated: "The wise are not learned; the learned are not wise."

A person 'knows', in fact, only because they are terrified of 'not knowing'. Knowledge must be recognized as 'insecure ignorance', which is why we prefer to harbor a thousand misconceptions rather than have no conceptions at all- because it is much easier to live with lies than to live without truths.

It is because of this, because we are more desperate to be sure than to be right, that our truths have become a pitiful compromise between the impossible admittance that we do not know, and the impossibility that we know.

Cioran concluded: "...this mind has squandered itself in what it has named and circumscribed."[38]

'Interpretation', then, is not- as our thought-based culture would have us believe- the absence of not-knowing, it is actually the hallmark of not-knowing; interpretation is the shuddering of the enigmaphobic; 'knowledge' is the shibboleth of pusillanimity.

"The stupid effort to drown your ignorance by false knowledge, is the only barrier between you and ...reality."
Osho[39]

---

38 *A Short History of Decay*, p7
39 *Ecstasy*, p128. As such, the metaphysical anarchist, Austin Osman Spare, admonishes: "Desiring to learn- think ye to escape hurt in the rape of your ignorance?" (*Anathema of Zos*)

By false thought we repress the only tool we have to honestly deal with the world- ignorance; for, by equating interpretation with understanding, we do not allow ourselves to not-understand, for we are hidden in the mist of thinking we understand.

What generally happens, however, is that when finally we begin to courageously divorce ourselves from the habit of interpretation, and we stick our heads out of our limited understanding, we suddenly see what we should have been seeing all along- the great Enigma waiting to engulf us. And because we have hidden behind the cowardly walls of interpretation for so long, we cannot now bear the vision of infinite mystery, and therefore we quickly spin about on our heels and crawl back into understanding.

Ernest Becker observed this symptom, writing: "...most of us- by the time we leave childhood- have repressed our vision of the primary miraculousness of creation. We have closed it off, changed it, and no longer perceive the world as it is to raw experience. ...The great boon of repression is that it makes it possible to live decisively in an overwhelmingly miraculous and incomprehensible world..."[40]

'Knowing', then, is repression; it is a 'functional delirium' of the mind, that is all; it is an effective illusion, which allows us to continue avoiding ourselves, avoiding the day when the dam will break and the river of Mystery will sweep us away for good.

Knowledge is nothing but ineffective nescience, or, imperfect ignorance. It is a way of looking at the world with only one eye open, and so it unfortunately it deceives us into believing that we fully can see.

John Van Druten states: "...for the most part we take for

---

40 *The Denial of Death*, p50

granted these things that are in fact the daily miracles of life, as we take for granted the miracle of growth and germination, scattering seeds in a garden and never being surprised that from those tiny black specks next summer's flowers can be relied upon to come."[41]

Interpretation, then, is a covering over the great bewildering immensity; a shell the turtle constructs around itself, to hide and blind itself within; a blanket, pulled between the child and darkness, blocking out the ubiquitous unknown.

"The intellectual attitude of our own time, so preponderantly antimythological, expresses our fear of the marvelous, for we have been trying to persuade ourselves that the universe is not a mystery, but a somewhat stupid machine."

Alan Watts[42]

There are no symbols adequate for what we attempt to symbolize; the more we describe the more we obscure. This is simply confusion gone mad.

"You know," declared J. Krishnamurti, "words are dangerous things because they are symbols, and symbols are not real."[43]

Words are unreal, because they are merely labels for the unknown; the *kun byed rgyal po'i mdo* explains: "...truth becomes evasive when its meaning should be expressed in

---

41 Introduction to *The Infinite Way*, by Joel Goldsmith, p10
42 *The Two Hands of God*, p11. Note here that 'machine' is the root of 'machination'.
43 Talks at Saanen (Aug. 1964). "Can you describe the perfume of a rose...? Can you tell how a kiss feels? Could you even describe the emotions of fear so that one who had not felt it, by former experience...would know what you meant?", asked Elsa Barker in *Letters From a Living Dead Man*, p264. And Carl Jung points out that an alchemical fiat of old runs: "*Rumpite ibros, ne corda vestra rumpantur* (Rend the books, lest your hearts be rent asunder)." (*Psychology and Alchemy*, p482)

words, and the mind's thinking is a total obstruction to truth. ...[Thus] if the nature of suchness...is not proclaimed with words and letters, the sentient beings with a capable mind will understand it, and thereby the nature of suchness will appear unveiled."[44]

And Sri Nisargadatta Maharaj, speaking from an equally rarified, metaphysical position, exclaimed, "Words are the mind and the mind obscures and distorts. Hence the absolute need to go beyond words. ...It is useless to struggle with words to express what is beyond words."[45]

Reality lies in the intimate experience of the mystery of existence, not in separation from the mystery, and yet separation arises inherently from the labeling of aspects of the one mystery.

As such, Thomas Carlyle argued: "What are your Axioms, and Categories, and Systems, and Aphorisms? Words, words. High Air-Castles are cunningly built of Words, the Words well bedded also in good Logic-mortar, wherein, however, no knowledge will come to lodge."[46]

---

44 p152,89. Realizing the decapitating effects of words, we can better understand U.G Krishnamurti's assertion: "You have never seen a tree, only your knowledge you have about trees. You see the knowledge, not the tree." (*Mind is a Myth*, p81) And using the same theme, the science-fiction and fantasy writer, Ursula K. LeGuin, describes her unique story *She Unnames Them* as such: "*She Unnames Them* is really an Adam and Eve story I subverted. Eve takes all the names back because they were either wrong from the start or they went wrong. As she does this, the barriers between herself and the world are dismantled. At the end of the story she has no words left...." LeGuin then goes on to state: "...we do use names to cut ourselves off. ...We manipulate names as categories of reality, and the names then become screens between ourselves and the world. The names become a tool of division rather than community. ...I know people who refuse to learn the names of trees- they have a concept of 'tree', but the names simply get between them and the real tree....We need to respect that some things are beyond names." (from *Whole Earth Review*, 1995)

45 *I AM THAT*, p154,104. And D.T. Suzuki states: "No amount of wordy explanations will ever lead us into the nature of our own selves. The more you explain, the further it runs away from you. It is like trying to get a hold of your own shadow. You run after it and it runs with you at the identical rate of speed." (*Essays in Zen Buddhism*, p22)

46 *Sartor Restorus*, p41. Carl Jung states: "Man's advance towards the Logos was a great achievement, but he must pay for it with loss of instinct and loss of reality to the degree

40

Indeed, it is not our ideas, interpretations, or judgements about 'suchness' which is the Reality, it is suchness itself, seen as it is, which is only possible by the naked mind.

Words are not 'suchness', or 'what is'; and thus words are dangerous because if that for which we have no clue we proceed to call 'this' or 'that', we forget that we have no clue. We have labeled the enigma and thus destroyed it. [47]

"No language can hope for anything but its own defeat."
Gregory Palamas[48]

Which is to say- what happens to 'what is', when we tangle our multifarious verse into the uni-verse, creating a multi-

---

that he remains in primitive dependence on mere words. Because words are substitutes for things, which of course they cannot be in reality, they take on intensified forms, become eccentric, outlandish, stupendous... neologisms tend not only to hypostatize themselves to an amazing degree, but actually to replace the reality they were intended to express. ...our submission to the tyranny of words [has] one great disadvantage: the conscious mind becomes more and more the victim of its own discriminating activity, the picture we have of the world gets broken down into countless particulars, and the original feeling of unity...is lost." (*Psyche and Symbol*, p246) And Joseph Campbell writes: "In fact, as I should think everyone must surely have discovered in his lifetime, it is actually impossible to communicate through speech any experience whatsoever, unless to someone who has himself enjoyed an equivalent experience of his own. Try explaining, for example, the experience of skiing down a mountain slope to a person who has never seen snow. Moreover, thoughts and definitions may annul one's own experiences even before they have been taken in: as, for instance, asking, "Can this that I feel be love?" "Is it allowed?" "Is it convenient?" Ultimately, of course, such questions may have to be asked, but the fact remains- alas!- that the moment they arise, spontaneity abates. Life defined is bound to the past, no longer pouring forward into the future. And, predictably, anyone continually knitting his life into contexts of intention, import, and clarifications of meaning will in the end find that he has lost the sense of experiencing life."(*Myths to Live By*, p133)

47 And so, according to Nietzsche, "We really ought to free ourselves from the misleading significance of words!" (*Beyond Good and Evil*)

48 This could be the reason why the genius maniac, William Burroughs, came to claim that language is a virus.

41

verse, and then attempt to collate our manifold symbols (which are not reality) into a 'way' of seeing- what happens is that we end up with a vision of life 'veiled' through lifeless symbols; life becomes a collage of dead, separate 'things', instead of a singular, flowing, living, wholeness[49]. This is why our term 'cata-logue' (*'cata-'*: destruction, and *'logos'*: the 'word') literally refers to the disaster that arises from collecting and organizing symbols, which is what happens when we compart-*mentalize* our understandings, and make closed, separate boxes, and so destroy the natural whole.

Concurring with this, Cioran injects: "Suppose we force ourselves to see to the bottom of words? We see nothing- each of them detached from the expansive and fertile soul, being null and void. The power of the intelligence functions by projecting a certain luster upon them, by polishing them and making them glitter; this power, erected into a system, is called culture-pyrotechnics against a night sky of nothingness."[50]

Words and facts are naught but veils over the wholeness and beauty of the mystery of ourselves, and of life.

"The more I know, the less I understand."
Don Henley

"If there was no language," concluded Swamiji Shyam,

---

49 Keeping this in mind we might better understand Dante's claim that- "Henceforth my vision mounted to a height where speech is vanquished and must lag behind"; a statement which arises not from the agony of the *Inferno* nor from the torpor of the *Purgatorio*, but instead from the ecstasy of his *Paradiso*.
50 *A Short History of Decay*, p20. And Osho stated this same idea, though perhaps in less nihilistic terms, writing: "All that your knowledge consists of is that you know a label. Forget the label and the unknown is there. All knowledge consists of only names. Drop the label and suddenly the unknown is there." (*Ecstasy*, p126)

"it would have been much better."[51]

It would have been much better because we would see ourselves as we are, not as words describe us. Words are the end of true understanding, just as true understanding is the end of words (by 'true understanding', I do not mean 'understanding' in the regular sense of the word- that is, as a synonym for 'knowing'- but rather in the humbler, more genuine, Taoist sense, which tends to locate us more realistically at our place amongst the immensity of the universe; which is to say, to truly understand is to 'stand under').

"The Tao which can be named is not the Tao."
Lao Tzu

Reality does not lie in facts, or names, or computations. These are but scars on the purity of the unnamable Life; just as white-noise, or disquieting sounds cover up the blessed silence, so also do arbitrary particularities obscure the unseparate, unknowable Absolute.[52]

Facts prevent us from perceiving the incomprehensible, singular spirit in all life, and instead create the dead, separate 'ten-thousand things' we have, to our detriment, been forced to

---

51 Talks, Apr 1998
52 "The Biblical story called 'The Tower of Babel' epitomizes man's ambition to change language from a means of self-expression into a tool for universal communication. The moral of this parable seems to imply a warning against man's presumptuous attempt to 'understand' everything by putting it into words. The fallacy of such an undertaking betrays itself in the vicious circle created by man who first named things in his own language, only to use the same language afterwards by which to 'explain' them. Thus it seemed easy to prove- be it in religious, sociological, or psychological terms- that this man-made universe was right. In reality, however, this creative ambition of man has produced ever-increasing confusion since the time of Babel..." Otto Rank (*Beyond Psychology*, p242)

erroneously learn, memorize, regurgitate, and function within, from the day of our birth onward.

The necessity, then, is not to further exert ourselves within the false paradigm, beating our heads against imaginary walls, or blinding ourselves even more with ideas, but instead to purge 'knowledge' from our consciousness of it, and walk right out of the diaphanous labyrinth.

We must simply break free now; we must stop understanding things the way we have been told to understand them.

Wonder is our escape route- our journey back to ourselves; wonder *is* life, the breath of the spirit itself; all else is tubercular boredom, consumption, suffocation, and stasis.

> ***"Sell your cleverness and buy bewilderment."***
> Rumi

It is our duty to ourselves to re-mystify the world, to steal it back from the thieves of wonder. Henry Miller described this vocation- to bring us back to the inescapable joy in the miracle of being- in one of his letters to Anais Nin. He wrote: "...a writer could completely baffle a psychologist; not only that, but that he was more of a psychologist than the other since he ramified the mysteries, extended them, developed them, and left the answers to go hang, because the answers weren't important, it was the drama, the mystery, the undecipherable pattern that was vital."

Our task is not to understand, but to return to perfect non-understanding, for truths are subtle atrocities by which we are unwittingly made falsely ignorant by false knowledge, and so we never have the expansive delight of vitalizing true ignorance.

Aldous Huxley remarked, "...the pleasures of ignorance

are as great, in their way, as the pleasures of knowledge."[53]

So we see that 'knowledge' obfuscates our unknowable life, because knowledge is impure ignorance; it is the smoke-screen of true ignorance, of the infinite freedom of awe, of liberating rapture.

We do not know what we are, we do not know why we are, we do not know who we are. We do not know! Let us finally, absolutely accept this, and begin to live again not as we think we are, but as we truly are, becoming like one of Clarice Lispector's emancipated characters, of whom she wrote: "... now that the layer of words had been removed from things, now that he had lost speech, he was finally standing in the calm depths of the mystery."[54]

The calm depths cannot be attained on the tempestuous surface. Without words, without labels, the world becomes naked and bare of the veil obscuring its authenticity, and though this effect is discomforting to the mind which requires things in little boxes, to the individual who has come to appreciate the value of 'innocent looking', so to speak, he or she finds that the world comes to make more sense ...because it makes less sense.

"The unintelligibility somehow makes profound sense."
Henry Miller.[55]

Somehow, it makes sense. And yet we do not know how. And we should not ask, for that was our mistake in the first place. No, we should be wise enough now simply to accept the

---

53 Karrie Kaszczuk adds, "Sometimes what we don't understand can be such a treasure, can't it?"
54 *The Apple in the Dark*, p109
55 *Sexus*, p214. Tertullian remarked: "*credo quia absurdum est*" (I believe, because it is absurd.)

implausibility of life, and neither retreat from it, nor try to solve it, but instead to sit back …and enjoy!

Lispector declared of her character again, "…[he] was wise enough not to know- and wise enough not to question, because he was a wise man now."[56]

We must learn again to understand with the mind of a person who knows that they do not understand; we must understand not-understanding, and then endure existing without a 'why?', without attempting a subterfuge around this.

"All I know is that I know nothing."
Socrates

Life lies waiting for us, and it is only the loss of our minds away. But we shall leave that for the next chapter. Let us end this one as we began, with Pooh:

"On Monday, when the sun is hot,
I wonder to myself a lot:
'Now is it true, or is it not,
That what is which and which is what?'

On Tuesday, when it hails and snows,
The feeling in me grows and grows
That hardly anybody knows
If those are these or these are those.

On Wednesday, when the sky is blue,
And I have nothing else to do,
I sometimes wonder if it's true

---

56 *The Apple in the Dark*, p317

That who is what and what is who."[57]

*****

---

57 *Winnie-the-Pooh*, by A.A. Milne

CHAPTER 3:
The Art of Forgetting, or, Epistemological Surrender

"For reality is the goal, deny it how we will. And we can approach it only by an ever-expanding consciousness, by burning more and more brightly, until even memory itself vanishes."
        Henry Miller [1]

"Was that, then, the way we do things? 'Not knowing?'- was that the way the most profound things happened? ...Was the secret of never escaping from the greater life the secret of living like a sleepwalker?"
        Clarice Lispector[2]

"It is not easy to destroy an idol: it takes as much time as is required to promote and to worship one. For it is not enough to annihilate its material symbol, which is easy; but its roots in the soul. How turn your eyes toward the twilight ages- where the past was liquidated under a scrutiny which only the void could dazzle...?"
        E.M. Cioran[3]

"So now we are going to investigate ourselves together...a journey of discovery into the most secret corners of our minds. And to take such a journey we must travel light; we cannot be burdened with opinions, prejudices, and conclusions. ...Forget all you know about yourself; forget all you have ever thought about yourself; we are going to start as if we knew nothing."
        Jiddu Krishnamurti[4]

---

1 *Wisdom of the Heart*, p46
2 *The Apple in the Dark*, p159
3 *A Short History of Decay*, p16
4 *Freedom from the Known*, p20

Now that we have witnessed the glories of rapture so easily destroyed by the irrelevancies of the mind, we must find a way to return ourselves to our once blessed state- a way to redeem our sacred spirits from the profanity of the day.

And how is this accomplished? How shall we undo, in one blinding second, what has taken a lifetime to build up? What is the task required of us in order to liberate ourselves from the shackles of lies, superfluities, misperceptions, and useless facts which merely cloud the purity of the rapturous mind? The task is simple: we need only reverse the process of our indoctrination; which is to say, the task is not to learn anything more, not to know anything more, not to remember anything more, but, on the contrary, the task is ...to forget.

"We must only be concerned with wiping away... "
J. Krishnamurti[5]

In the end, it is not what we accept inside ourselves that matters, but what we eschew; in order to purge the taint from within, we must simply learn to 'unknow' ourselves and everything at every moment. We must rise out of context, out of the current paradigm, out of any idea we harbor of life, the world, or ourselves, for, as we shall see as this chapter unfolds, emancipation happens to us not from gain, but ...from loss.

Friedrich Nietzsche declared: "The Will to Truth, which is to tempt us to many a hazardous enterprise, the famous, Truthfulness of which all philosophers have hitherto spoken with respect, what questions has this Will to Truth not laid before us! What strange, perplexing, questionable questions! It is already a

5 Talks in Bombay, Mar 1961

long story; yet it seems as if it were hardly commenced. Is it any wonder if we at last grow distrustful, lose patience, and turn impatiently away? ...[Now] we are learning *to forget and not know*...we have got disgusted with this bad-taste, this will-to-truth, to 'truth at all costs', this youthful madness in the love of truth; we are now too experienced for that..."[6]

The simple fact is that we cannot be tangled in the ubiquitous web of delusions which the mind is akin to, and also be free. Hence the need is not to set about trying to understand our confines- because 'understanding' *is* our confines; we must not strive to know ourselves through the methods and jargon given to us, we must instead release those methods and all of their previous findings. We must extract ourselves from the lie of context.

"You must unlearn that which you have learned."
Yoda[7]

To turn towards the bald, innocent, immobilizing unfathomableness, without any direction, guidance, or expectation; to forget everything anyone has ever said- to stop looking for meaning, to remember nothing every instant, that is when the true life of wonder and miracle will again come upon us- when we abandon all knowledge of ourselves, when we lose the ability to recall perspective- when we forget everything.

Chuang Tzu relates a brief anecdote: "I am learning," Yen Hui said. "How?" the Master said. "I forgot the rules of

---

6 *Beyond Good and Evil*, p1; *The Joyful Wisdom*, p9
7 *Return of the Jedi*, by George Lucas. This same thought was expressed by the astrophysicist, Patrick Côté, who unequivocally stated, "You have to learn to unlearn" and Osho, who wrote, "It is not a question of learning much. On the contrary, it is a question of unlearning much." (*Ecstasy*, p12),

Righteousness and the levels of Benevolence," he replied. "Good, but could be better," the Master said. A few days later, Yen Hui remarked, "I am making progress." "How?" the Master asked. "I forgot the Rituals and the Music," he answered. "Better, but not perfect," the Master said. Some time later, Yen Hui told the Master, "Now I sit down and forget everything." The Master looked up, startled. "What do you mean, you forget everything?" he quickly asked. "I forget my body and senses, and leave all appearance and information behind," answered Yen Hui. "In the middle of Nothing, I join the Source of All Things." The Master bowed. "You have transcended the limitations of time and knowledge. I am far behind you. You have found the Way!"

It is through the emptiness that comes about from forgetting that we are returned to the great enigmatic whole. Or, more precisely, it is not we who are returned to the whole, the whole simply emerges- due to our absence; the whole, arises out of the hole.

Perhaps a little more information will clarify the matter. Let us dig deeper into this 'forgetting' business.

By 'forgetting' I am not speaking simply about the momentary loss of some object, or the name of some person, I am speaking of absolute amnesia, of a state where everything we thought we were, and everything we thought life was suddenly dissolves (dis-*solves*) away, and we are left with a blank-slate. We are gone completely, now and forever.[8]

---

8 It is no strange occurrence that the Eastern word '*Nirvana*'- for which the soppy romanticism of the Occident has strategically branded as the equivalent to our Elysium fields (lousy with busty maidens and champagne streams)- is, in fact, most literally translated into the English word 'desperation': which is to say, an ex-piration, or, 'blowing out' of the garbage from the mind; a getting-rid-of all that is within. Hence 'Nirvana' is not a place, but is instead a space- a complete absence; it is complete inward emptiness, or poverty, as it were (just as Utopia can mean: a place that is nowhere). That is why the word 'redemption' contains the word 'empty'; for it is only when we become empty of all concepts and 'identities' that we become a hole, creating from our absence a

This essential fact is outlined in the anonymously written, unorthodox, mystical tract on wonder, *The Cloud of Unknowing*, which seeks to return us to our highest stature, not by coming to 'know' God, but by 'unknowing' everything. It states: "Well, where is the hard work then? Without a doubt it is in the stamping out all remembrance of God's creation, and in keeping them covered by that cloud of forgetting... [For] if ever you are to come to this...cloud of unknowing [in which God exists]... you must also put a cloud of forgetting beneath you and all creation."[9]

To enter into the 'cloud of unknowing' first we must go through the 'cloud of forgetting' which requires us to totally leave the known, which means we must leave ourselves (or at least the sense which we now have of ourselves).

We must disappear without remainder. Nothing must be left of what we thought the world was, or who we thought we were; to forget, is to forget everything. Everything. It is a death. The mind must be abandoned completely.

"Surrender is an act of humility, an acknowledgement that life is a mystery whose depth the mind cannot fathom."
Dan Millman[10]

We must surrender the knowledge we have been given, we must die to our own perspectives, we must die to any conclusion, assumption, presumption, or idea about anything we

---

holy whole; in the act of forgetting, a vacuum occurs- an opening in the universe- in which the creation is swallowed back into the Creator. Blessed, indeed, are the poor in spirit, as the first beatitude suggests- for they alone shall be truly empty, and in being truly empty of falsehood, they may eventually be filled.
9 p94,66
10 *The Laws of Spirit*, p96

have ever had; we must die to the idea of ourselves. Only than shall we be empty, unknown, unknowing, and free.

Cioran announced: "To get back to the source of these expressions of the vague, we must make an affective regression toward their essence, must drown in the ineffable and emerge from it with our concepts in tatters. Once our theoretical assurance and our pride in the intelligible is lost, we can try to understand everything for itself. Then we manage to rejoice in the inexpressible, to spend our days in the margin of the comprehensible, and to wallow in the suburbs of the sublime. In order to escape sterility, we must wear Reason's mourning..."[11]

We must forfeit what we believe is our treasure. We must give up what we claim is our need. There is nothing we need to know, but everything we need to unknow. We must lighten the load if we are to fly.

The only way to return to the Mystery is to detach ourselves from the context of unmystery; to wipe the slate clean, over and over again, and to never get caught in the static drawing. This is to become completely ignorant of what we thought life was, or is, to lose all concepts, and to ease back through ignorance to the unimaginable Source of all that is.[12]

---

11 *A Short History of Decay*, p31. A parallel observation to this comes from Bede Griffith's wonderful book, *The Marriage of East and West*: "We are all pilgrims in search of truth, or reality, of fulfillment. But we have to recognize that this Truth will always remain beyond our understanding. No science or philosophy or theology can ever encompass the Truth. No poetry or art or human institution can ever embody it. The great Myths are only reflections in the human imagination of that transcendental Mystery. ...we have to go beyond the Myth to the Mystery itself, beyond word and thought, beyond life and death. ...No imaginative vision or conceptual framework is adequate to the great reality." (p203-204)

12 Here I am broaching upon the subtle metaphysic of Oneness; i.e. when the separate individual consciously rejoins the One Consciousness from which, due to delusion, the individual had thought themselves to be set apart. However, to lose the knowledge which created the separate 'ten thousand things', is to create a whole in which you yourself belong, for when the mind is wiped clean of distinction, only the One great mystery remains, and nothing exists outside of it. Thus Pierre Tielhard de Chardin claimed that "Purity does not lie in separation from but in deeper penetration into the universe... The

"It is only when we discard all knowledge
that we begin to know."
Henry David Thoreau

We then begin to 'know', though not in a conceptual, intellectual way, but rather in a more intimate, experiential, holistic, indefinable way; for conventional 'knowing' is ever confined to a limited perspective and cannot of itself encompass the whole.

Life, then, has more redemptive power as the Great Mystery (i.e. it returns us to our true selves) only when we see it truly, as it is- the one, great, all-inclusive enigma.

When finally we forget the false way of knowing ourselves and everything, and wake up (again) to the fact that we know nothing- that is when existence returns to its authentic state, and we return to our authentic way of 'being'.[13]

---

world is filled and filled with the [unknowable] Absolute. To see this is to be made free." And U.G. Krishnamurti asserted that: "Once thought has burnt itself out, nothing that creates division can remain there."(*Mind is a Myth*, p77) That is: the moment you cease trying to find an answer, duality comes to an end; for duality is the outcome of the ambitious mind (*ambi-*: two. i.e. the desire, or ambition, to understand *creates* the duality of otherness). Eckhart Tolle explains this as such: "Identification with your mind creates an opaque screen of concepts, labels, images, words, judgements, and definitions that blocks the true relationship. It comes between you and yourself, between you and your fellow man and woman, between you and nature, between you and God. It is this screen of thought that creates the illusion of separateness, that illusion that there is you *and* a totally separate 'other'. You then forget the essential fact that, underneath the level of physical appearances and separate forms, you are one with all that *is*." (*The Power of Now*, p13) And that one, is one mystery.

13 Joseph Campbell describes here a practice for forgetting. He writes: "The yogi is to penetrate and cast aside (as a serpent sloughs its skin) the whole spectacle of phenomenality- forms, names, and relationships- letting only that which shines through all as undifferentiated consciousness remain to his contemplation. ...Pick up, for example, any object at all. Draw mentally a ring around it, setting it off from the world. Forgetting its use, forgetting its name, not remembering that it was made or how, or that

Jean Paul Sartre expressed this process, exultantly confessing: "I couldn't remember...any more. The words had vanished, and with them, the significance of things, their methods of use, and the feeble points of reference men have traced on their surface. ...It left me breathless. Never, until these last few days, had I understood the meaning of *existence*. I was like the others. ...I said with them: The ocean is green, that the white speck up there is a seagull, but I didn't feel that it existed. ...And then suddenly existence had unveiled itself."[14]

Existence 'unveils' itself, when we lift the veil of our preconception- when we forget how we used to view the world.

> *"To attain knowledge, add things every day.*
> *To attain wisdom, remove things every day."*
> Lao Tzu

Freedom comes from a form of creative decomprehension; there is no valid symbology, understanding, nor thought which cannot not be gotten-out-of (i.e. escaped from, thus 'unveiling' existence in its nude reality) by acontextual intent; we are released from the trap of the mind by the unharnessable freedom of unknowing; we are released from our bondage by re-cognizing life as it truly is- inconceivable.

Complete ignorance is the only unbiased, unhindered cognition, producing the 'no mind' inherently necessary for the window of wonder to re-open; in such ignorance everything

---

names are given to its parts; not knowing *what* it is, but only *that* it is, simply regard it; and so then: What *is* it? ...Anything at all, any stick, stone, cat, or bird, dissociated from every concept this way, will be seen as a wonder without 'meaning'... For contemplating it thus we are thrown back upon our own pure state, as subject to an object, each then the aspect of a mystery 'thus come'." (*The Mythic Image*, p305)
14 *La Nausee*, p170

filters through the new openness, for there are no longer walls; the individual is redeemed back to unity through the spaciousness of their limitless mind. Which is to say- Absolution is ...the absence of solution.[15]

Lispector arrived at the same conclusion in one of her articles, when she wrote: "...there comes a moment of revelation about life, about myself, about others, about true art, and a sudden awareness that even the greatest of abstractions are not really abstract. The only drawback about such moments is that I forget them almost immediately. As if this were our pact with God: to see and forget rather than be struck down by knowledge."[16]

It is our need, our right, our privilege, and our duty to forget; though it is a vocation that gains us no wealth, success, nor applause. And yet it is the task of every earnest person, consumed with the affinity for reality- at all costs. And the cost is ...everything; every scrap of belief, assumption, hope, or concern. In the end we cannot even take our worries with us, for these also are born from the mind, and these also must die with it.

"I maintain that your natural state is one of 'not knowing'."
U.G. Krishnamurti[17]

We must learn to constantly do-away-with, so as to constantly be living in the equilibrium of awe- which is intimate,

---

15 This point will also be further expanded upon in the chapter dealing with the theological history of the Occident, specifically Christianity, its concept of the Fall, and of sin. Suffice it to say for now that it is only because we "claim to know" that we are "guilty of sin"- as it is suggested in the gospels.
16 *Jorno do Brasil*, May24/6
17 *Mind is a Myth*, p75

in-tune-with, and aware of life's inherent brilliance. This is the hallmark of forever confronting the unknown within, and all around us.

As the directives from *The Cloud of Unknowing* continue: "Be willing to be blind, and give up all longing to know the why and how, for knowing will be more of a hindrance than a help."[18]

It is therefore essential that the individual 'unknow' what he or she 'knows', ceaselessly abandoning the myth of knowing. The mind must learn to exorcise its contents at every moment, or it will continually be full when it should be perpetually empty.

Passages from the ancient *kun byed rgyal po'i mdo* continue this point: "...investigation and meditation are particularly pointless [for realizing] the manifestation of truth...and...the self-originating pristine awareness. ...If no [theoretical framework] is applied...mind will shine forth as [it has been] from the beginning. ...The eye which sees the no-object, sees the wonder. ...Who separate themselves from what they hear and what people talk about, they will remain in a state of union with things and Reality, and will be inseparable from them." [brackets are translator's][19]

We must leave no stone unturned, nor any scraps of truth remaining by which the vain and deluded mind might sustain itself. We must forget what we are not, if ever we are to be what we truly are.

A comment by the Sufi Hazrat Inayat Kahn expands upon this theme: "All ideas have been learned from one source or another; yet in time one comes to think they are one's own. And for those ideas a person will argue and dispute, although they do not satisfy him fully; but at the same time they are his

18 p101
19 p105,95,106

battleground, and they will continue to keep his cup covered. Mystics therefore have adopted a different way. They have learned a different course, and that course is self-effacement, or in other words, unlearning what one has learned; and this is how one can become an empty cup... One may think that in this way one loses one's individuality; but what is individuality? Is it not what is collected? What are one's ideas and opinions? They are just collected knowledge, and this knowledge should be unlearned."[20]

J. Krishnamurti concurred with this idea, stating: "Thought can never bring about innocency and humility and yet it is innocency and humility that keep the mind young, sensitive, incorruptible. Freedom from the known is the ending of thought; to die to thought, from moment to moment, is to be free from the known. It is this death that puts an end to decay."[21]

Such is the case, that if we are to transform, like the butterfly, first we must enter the darkened cocoon as a confused, suffering, shivering, caterpillar; we must die to the tantalizing light, if ever we are to grow wings, break free, leave the ground, and fly.

"Here is manifest how the Way of Life is found only through a Death, and that, without the deprival of all other knowledge, Self-Knowledge itself is not to be achieved."
Hermetica[22]

We must lose our balance in the world, grasping onto none of the holds that are bound to the limited, conceptual world.

20 *The Mysticism of Music, Sound, and Word*, p150
21 *Notebooks*, p180
22 quoted in Lindsay Clarke's *Chymical Wedding*, p221

We must burn clean-through.

This threshold was crossed by Blaise Pascal who described himself as such: "I know not who put me into this world, nor what the world is, nor what I am myself. I am in terrible ignorance of everything..." Here, in Pascal, we have a leading scientific and theological mind, humbly confessing to his total loss of grasp on the meaning of life, and yet that loss was the very wellspring of his inspirations and writings.

To develop this 'consciousness of our ignorance', is simply a matter of recognizing the profundity of being, of accepting that what we thought we knew is merely a smoke screen, a 'fog of words', blinding us to its immensity.

Osho speaks to this essential recognition, proffering: "You know that nothing can be known, you know that ignorance is primordial, you know that life is a mystery and is going to remain a mystery, and you know that truth is not only unknown but unknowable. You are freed from the illusion of knowledge."[23]

And so we must undo what has been done to us, and the only way to undo it is to forget; to become innocent again, to disappear from our own sight, for the further we continue to imbibe more facts, theories, and conclusions, the more, in the end, we will have to purge from ourselves in order to return to purity, innocence, and emptiness, which is our inherent nature.

"Because the human scene is entirely a misconception through misperception, any thought...must be relinquished in order that we may see the ever-present Reality."
Joel Goldsmith[24]

---

23 *Ecstasy*, p136
24 *The Infinite Way*, p33

Thus the attainment of ignorant wonderfulness is more a matter of ejecting the mind's effluvium than of any effortful accumulation of understanding. All we need to do is be stoically aware of the impotence of the mind; to simply and completely accept that we do not understand the greater part of who, or what, or why we are.

It is merely a matter of understanding that we do not understand, that is all.

> *"To study ourselves is to forget ourselves."*
> Dogen

That is, to study ourselves is to dis-recognize ourselves.[25]

The more we look into ourselves with sedulous, blank honesty, the more we lose the words we were given to describe ourselves; and the more we step out of our everyday habits and perceptions, the more we realize we have no clue about ourselves, except that we suddenly become a greater and greater mystery continually, at every moment. That is when we begin to see ourselves truly.

Sri Nisargadatta Maharaj stated: "You give reality to concepts, while concepts are distortions of reality. Abandon all conceptualization and stay silent and attentive. ...[For] the spirit touches matter and consciousness results. Such consciousness, when tainted with memory and expectation, becomes bondage. Pure experience does not bind... Self-forgetting is inherent in

---

25 Similarly, Abu-Said suggests, "To be a Sufi is to detach from fixed ideas...to put away what is in your head- imagined truth, preconceptions, conditioning..." (quoted in *The Way of the Sufi* by Idries Shaw, p239)

self-knowing... Free from memory and expectation, I am fresh, innocent, and wholehearted."[26]

And Samuel Beckett synopsized this realization nicely when he wrote: "All has proceeded all this time in the utmost calm, the most perfect order...the meaning of which escapes me. No, it is not that their meaning escapes me, my own escapes me just as much. ...Dear incomprehension, it's thanks to you I'll be myself, in the end."[27]

"Because I know I shall not know."
T.S. Eliot[28]

To be ourselves- that is the only thing we are after. It is very simple, and very hard. We open ourselves up by forgetting, we forget ourselves by studying ourselves, and we study ourselves by letting go of the mind and its shackles- by seeing life new again, without praise, disdain, right, wrong, bias, judgement, or expectation. "The mind which is not crippled by memory has real freedom", declared Jiddu Krishnamurti.[29]

And thus "The loss of memory," admitted Anais Nin, "was like the loss of a chain. With all this fluidity came a great lightness. Without memory I was immensely light, vaporous, fluid. The memory was the density which I could not transcend..."[30]

Kahn describes this experience as such: "A really musical soul is someone who has forgotten himself in music; just as a real poet is someone who forgets himself in poetry, and a

26 *I AM THAT*, p154,100,93,86
27 *Malloy, Malone Dies, The Unnameable*
28 *Ash Wednesday*
29 *Freedom from the Known*, p36
30 *The Voice*, p51

worldly soul is someone who has lost himself in the world. And godly is the soul who has forgotten himself in God. ...[Such individuals] altogether lost the idea of their own being, and in that way they deepened and became one with the thing they had come to give to the world. The key to perfection is to be found in forgetting the self."[31]

Every step of this re-awakening is death, but only the death of facts and labels, and these are already dead. Courageously dying in the mind is the only way to re-create an opening for the true and the real to occur, for nothing new will ever be born from a lie.

What we have called 'knowing' is so thoroughly erroneous that the only truth lies in the absence of all we know, not in the addition of further facts.

Writing about one of her characters, Clarice Lispector delivers one of her subtle observations about this process, stating: "Then by means of a very familiar lack of comprehension the man at last began to be himself in an indistinct sort of way."[32]

To be ourselves is to know nothing. In such a state of unworrying acceptance of 'being', without 'doing' anything about it, there it is that we shall find and be ourselves uninhibitedly.

"My dearest, you may recite or listen to countless scriptures, but you will not be established within until you can forget everything."
Astavakra Gita (16.1)

---

31 *The Mysticism of Music, Sound, and Word*, p136. Kahn's fellow countryman, Rabidrinath Tagore exclaimed similarly, "Drunk with joy of singing I forget myself and call thee friend who art my lord." (*Gitanjali*, II)
32 *The Apple in the Dark*

To become established is to 'know that you shall not know', it is to find and be the true mystery which we are, which is to accept our incomprehension without a shred of doubt, and to give ourselves up to the enigma of life completely, more completely, in fact, than if we knew all and everything from the moment we were born. Genius is not that which claims to know, but that which recognizes the unknowability of being. And the genius of our beings is 'established' when we take firm root in idiocy.

Henry Miller concluded his personal path when he wrote: "I grow more ignorant every day- purposely so!"[33]

To purposely 'grow more ignorant'? This sounds like shooting yourself in the foot. You'd have to be a complete idiot to attempt something like that. But, then again, that is the goal we are after here- to become complete, lucid idiots.

> *"Keep forgetting and don't remember anything.*
> *It can happen."*
> Swamiji Shyam[34]

As such, Clarice Lispector described her character's

---

33 *Hamlet Letters*
34 By forgetting the forgettable we re-member the real Being, and we become eternally 'established' in place of the evanescence of the unreal being. This outcome is described from another angle by Shunry Suzuki, who states: "And we should not hoard knowledge; we should be free from our knowledge. If you collect various pieces of knowledge, as a collection it may be very good, but this is not our way. We should not try to surprise people by our wonderful treasures. We should not be interested in something special. If you want to appreciate something fully, you should forget yourself. You should accept it like lightning flashing in the utter darkness of the sky. ...We should always live in the dark empty sky. The sky is always the sky. Even though clouds and lightning come, the sky is not disturbed. Even if the flashing of enlightenment comes, our practice forgets all about it." (*Zen Mind, Beginner's Mind.* p85-86)

iconoclastic idiocy, stating, "And soon, with the great pleasure that there is in the restraint of one's own energy, he put himself once more into a state of 'not knowing very much.'"[35]

'To forget', then, requires only the desire to forget. We must have intent to undo. We must be the cleaners of the internal mess. We must be the fire which sunders everything to ash, and leaves a perfect hollow.

> *"And I pray that I may forget*
> *these matters that with myself*
> *I too much discuss*
> *Too much explain."*
> T.S. Eliot

It is simply a matter of how serious we are; whether we really are willing to die as caterpillars, so that we might fly away as butterflies.

The truth of the matter is that to forget is to lose without thought of gain, and to gain without thought of loss. For the only thing we ever lose is the memory of what 'has been', we never lose the moment, for the moment always 'is', and it is our task to make each moment more and more important, more and more real, and the only way to do that is to lose all sight of the past, to discard the baggage we carry, to regain spontaneity, to see 'what is' as it is, not as it has been in the past.

U.G Krishnamurti adds to this categorical necessity; of this intent, he declares: "My motive is direct and temporary; ...I am only interested in making it crystal clear that *there is nothing to understand.* ...As long as you think, accept, and believe that there is something to understand, and make that understanding a

---

35 *The Apple in the Dark*, p91

goal to be placed before you, demanding search and struggle, you are lost and will live in misery. ...So...there is the actual need to be free from answers themselves. The search is invalid because it is based upon questions which in turn are based upon false knowledge. Your knowledge has not freed you from your problems. ...So freedom exists not in finding answers, but in the dissolution of all questions." [36]

Infinity lies waiting for us to perceive it, we must only polish the lens first in order to not see what is not there.

This is the *via negativa* path, the abandonment of all the mind's securities, the jettisoning-over of all that we think we are, of all that we could, or should, or want to be, and thus falling back faithfully into the great sea of awe and unmeaning. Only then shall we be empty of conventional knowledge, open, pure, innocent, capacious, and ready for the impossible.

"The knowledge beyond knowledge is my knowledge."
Kabir

We begin to live completely in the moment, and in the mystery, without the hindrance of 'what?', 'how?', or 'why?', when we are free of the need to know.

We are infinite just as we are, only we are clogged with the detritus of all we are not.

And so we must "cleanse the doors of perception", as William Blake suggested, and this requires cleansing the mind, for only in doing so do we re-awaken to life's novelty and allow Beauty to flow uninhibitedly through us.

Thus Nietzsche was able to claim: "...the blissful ecstasy that arises from the innermost depths of man, ay, of nature, at

---

36 *Mind is a Myth*, p91-92

this same collapse of the *principium individuationis*...[is] an insight into the Dionysian, which is brought into closest ken, perhaps, by the analogy of drunkenness. It is either under the influence of the narcotic draught, of which the hymns of all primitive men and peoples tell us, or by the powerful approach of Spring penetrating all nature with joy, that the Dionysian emotions awake, in which the subject vanishes in complete forgetfulness."[37]

*****

---

37 *The Birth of Tragedy*, p26. Speaking of this Dionysian styled drunkenness, one of Omar Khyam's quatrains runs: "I drink not for joy of wine/ nor to scoff at faith/ but only to forget myself for a while./ That alone is my want of intoxication, that alone." (*The Rubaiyat of Omar Khyam*)

CHAPTER 4:
Organic Mysticism, or, The Tao of Ignorance

"...one thing became very clear and that was that there were ways of not understanding and that the difference between the non-understanding of one individual and the non-understanding of another created a world of terra firma even more solid than differences of understanding."
    Henry Miller[1]

"The man had expected nothing and he saw what he saw, as if he had not been made to draw conclusions but just to look."
    Clarice Lispector[2]

"...I contemplate the spasm of ideas, while the Void smiles at itself."
    E.M. Cioran[3]

"Clarity is essential. I mean by 'clarity', seeing things as they are, seeing the 'what is', without any opinion, seeing the movement of your mind, observing it very closely, minutely, diligently, without any purpose, without any directive."
    Jiddu Krishnamurti[4]

---

1 *Tropic of Capricorn*, p220
2 *The Apple in the Dark*, p78
3 *A Short History of Decay*, p104
4 Talks in Madras, 1964

The need to forget the unmiraculous ideas we have been taught, in order to see the pristine miracle of existence once again, is easy to accept. The question that remains, however, is how do we go about 'forgetting'? What must we do in order to clear away the dross and let the true gold shine through? And the answer, oddly enough, is: nothing.

There is no methodology which might direct us toward reality, for all methodologies are based upon action within a 'known' forum, and it is this 'known' which is itself the door which we must unknow in order to walk through.[5]

Thus organic mysticism is not about 'finding', 'becoming', 'achieving', 'transcending', or 'understanding', it is simply about *being*; nor is it about meditation, prayer, austerities, or pilgrimages, for in order to be with the mystery, we do not have to do anything, except *be*.

"The greatest art is like stupidity."
Chuang Tzu

Organic mysticism is not about rites, mantras, dogmas, or spiritual exercises (all of which, though perhaps valid in their own context, eventually become limiting factors to absolute unknowing, specifically because they do require context in order to be valid), it is about looking honestly at ourselves and everything, about de-identifying ourselves with the 'I' which participates in the play of being; it is about looking upon the self

---

5 That is, since we have learned initially to view the world completely incorrectly, if we then choose to participate in any conceptual way within this wrong paradigm we simply end up validating it, when it should instead be invalidated; it is our re-action to falsity, in any manner whatsoever, that binds us more completely into falsehood, moreso than if we were instead to be passively conscious of its invalidity and nothing more.

as if for the very first time, and letting it go, over and over again, so that *It* might continue to be and become more Itself, never again to be bound by the limiting mind.

Regarding the non-necessity of disciplines and directives, Franz Kafka stated, in unabashed reflection: "Self control is something for which I do not strive. Self control means: wanting to work effectively at some random point in the infinite radiations of my spiritual existence. But if I must draw such circles round me, then it will be better for me to do it passively, merely gaping in wonder at the immense complex, and just take home with me the strength which this spectacle, *e contrario*, provides."[6]

To attain this 'passivity' we must live without thought of reward, goal, or attainment. We must exist in the world without knowing what it is to exist in the world. We must detach from our petty needs and understandings; we must effortlessly watch ourselves with complete, objective detachment, as if we were watching someone else watching someone else.

Zen Master Fenyang relates this finding, suggesting: "When you're settled...your mind is serene, unaffected by worldly distractions. You enter the realm of enlightenment, and transcend the ordinary world, leaving the world while in the midst of society."[7]

He is pointing to the 'no mind', spoken of in Zen training, which implies absolute, unadulterated, innocent, novel, effortless attention.

Seeing is not a function only of the eyes, it is a mind-set; whether we look through given interpretations and filters, or instead take them off and see clearly with nothing in between us and life; whether we choose to polish the lenses or continue to see 'through a glass darkly'; or whether we choose to smash the

---

6 *On Sin, Suffering, and the True Way*
7 *Zen Essence*, p16

windows, and let the breeze of brilliance blow through.

"You needn't seek wonders, for wonders come of themselves."
Zen Master Lingi

Mystery *is*, it need not be invoked nor sought after, it need only be recognized.

The glory of being cannot help but spontaneously appear when our vision is clear enough to see it. Acknowledging this, the *kun byed rgyal po'i mdo* claims: "The great wonders are not difficult [to see]. Through subtleness the understanding of suchness as to all good qualities and forces immediately arises from its own"[8]

I am pointing to the natural outcome of honest perception, which leads to the realization of incomprehension, which leads to awe, which leads to life. Wonderment is simply the initial gust, the shock that occurs when all the lenses are cleared- the inaugural, flabbergasting startlement that 'what is' IS! It is the annihilation of all previous premises, prejudices, and pseudo-profundities. When we finally look completely at ourselves and the world, for the very first time, we shall see the wordless, unimaginable, intimate, inimitable miracle of being blossoming all around and within us.

And for this we do not have to seek for some secret, or develop great spiritual talents; we do not have to do anything, life does it all, for the essence of life *is* its unknowability.

"The true mystery of the world is the visible, not the invisible", observed Oscar Wilde. Which is to say- the unknown *is* the known, and the known *is* the unknown; the Mystery stands right before us and in us, we need only open our minds and let

8 p118

this realization surge in.

Life is an unimaginable miracle. Nothing is plausible. Nothing.

"To exist is a state as little conceivable as its contrary. No, still more inconceivable."
E.M. Cioran[9]

Thus there is no process involved in true seeing, there is no 'understanding' which becomes obvious, there is only a meaninglessness of incredible meaning that lies waiting to be uncovered in all and everything. Mystery becomes the way to itself, because there is naught but mystery.

It is simply a matter of focus, of contracting and expanding, of plying the extent of our sight, of accepting that we cannot focus upon two distances at once, of intentionally blurring what is now clear, so that what is blurred may emerge clearly in plain view.

This is a facile reversal of cognition, a subtle return to the purity which has not been lost but only buried beneath the mire, for the truth is that we contain everything necessary to experience wonder, because ...nothing is necessary.

Osho remarks: "Nature is enough... No imposed laws and disciplines are needed. Innocence is enough. No morality is needed. Nature is spontaneous, nature is enough. No imposed laws and disciplines are needed. Innocence is enough. Knowledge is not needed. ...the real guru is life itself. ...[Therefore] just be, moment to moment, not knowing who you are...and what you are."[10]

---

9 *The Trouble With Being Born*, p104
10 *Book of Secrets; Ecstasy*, p35

Life is enough unto itself; to 'be' is, in its absolute essence, an ineffable, inexpressible, inexhaustible event of beauty and strangeness; the staggering aspect of 'being' is *that* it is, and that it is thoroughly incomprehensible.

Excerpts from the *kun byed rgyal po'i mdo*, continue to address this view: "It is a path, subtle and difficult to understand, which is non-speculative and beyond thinking. It is non-existent, imperceptible, and non-conceptual, it is free of all thinking. It cannot be captured in words, free from form and color, it is not an object of the sense faculties. It is firm, difficult to comprehend, and totally inexplicable. ...Through an attitude free of desires...nature is self-perfected. ...and there is no need for [certain] activities, as likewise, the essentials are unagitated, and therefore don't need to be achieved. ...It is a natural knowledge, broad and without boundaries or a center. ...There is no becoming as everything is just as it is. ...A practitioner...who abides in a state of non-conceptual thinking and who [thinks] 'whatever is, is right', this person manifests the [highest]... intention. ...There is nothing else than abiding...in balance, without conceptual thinking. ...There is no need to carry out meditation as Reality is oneself. Do not seek a place of meditation, do not depend on others. ...and do not try to understand intellectually the imperceptible nature. Do not search for Reality in anything else than yourself."[11]

Organic mysticism (I call it organic mysticism, but the only real name for it is ...life. I am not espousing a new religion, merely the abandonment of all that is old) is a natural process, it is not a function of cultivation, examination, manipulation, or adaptation. It is the realization that asceticisms, prostrations, petitions, sacrifices, and self-denials are wholly unnatural.

---

11 p112,100,112,109,163,101,149,150

"That the world is, is the mystical."
Ludwig Wittgenstein[12]

Recognizing this means, again, that no efforts or achievements will change anything, in fact they may take us farther away from our true selves, and farther from reality, because these actions, bound into erroneous paradigms, run wholly against the grain of our wonder-full beings.

Osho implores us onward: "My sannyas [i.e. practice] is spontaneity, living moment to moment without any prefabricated discipline, living with the unknown, not exactly knowing where you are going. Because if you already know where you are going you are dead. Then life runs in a mechanical way. A life should be a flow from the known towards the unknown. One should be dying each moment to the known so the unknown can penetrate you. And only the unknown liberates. ...live a life of spontaneity, of nature. Don't try to corrupt your future. Let it be...don't try to manage it. Don't give it a mold and a form and a pattern. ...Remain unprepared, then you will be excited, then each moment will be a joy and a wonder, and each moment will bring something new to you which has never happened, and you will never be bored. ...Move in freedom, move in total freedom, and each moment remember to drop the past. ...Just go on ceasing as far as the past is concerned, dying as far as the past is concerned, so you are totally alive, throbbing, pulsating, streaming..."[13]

This 'amethodological methodology' of aconceptual existence is simply the unshackling of the imprisoned mind- of loosing the conceptual grip we have unwittingly placed upon

---

12 quoted in *Zen to Go*, p119
13 *Ecstasy*, p39-43. Thus "To be natural" wrote John O'Donohue, "is to be holy; but it is very difficult to be natural. To be natural is to be at home with your own nature. If you are outside your self, always reaching beyond your self, you avoid the call of your own mystery." (*Anam Cara*, p133)

ourselves. That is when realization leads to unrealization, decay turns into growth, and without struggle or skill we become our true marvelous selves, agog in the spellbinding universe, simply because reality itself is fantastically outrageous already.

*"I do not understand. That phrase is so overwhelming that it transcends any understanding. Our understanding is always limited. But not to understand can be without frontiers. I feel myself much more complete when I do not understand.
Not to understand, in the sense I mean, is a gift."*
Clarice Lispector[14]

The ability to receive the givenness of the miracle of life is the gift; life remains the same event either way- whether we see it as a burden or a blessing- it is simply our reception which determines which side of the coin we are on.

Sri Nisargadatta Maharaj offers his opinion, observing: "What is the use of truth, goodness, harmony, beauty? They are their own goal. They manifest spontaneously and effortlessly, when things are left to themselves, are not interfered with, not shunned, or wanted, or conceptualized, but just experienced in full awareness. [This] awareness...does not make use of things and people- it fulfills them. ...I follow no rules nor lay down rules. I flow with life- faithfully and irresistibly. ...Just live your life as it comes, but alertly, watchfully, allowing everything to happen as it happens, doing the natural things the natural way, suffering, rejoicing- as life brings. ...You agree to be guided from within and life becomes a journey into the unknown."[15]

---

14 *JdoB*, Feb1/69
15 *I AM THAT*, p14,115,19,33. Similarly, Alan Watts claimed: "You never have to hold onto it. If you feel that, then realize that the movement of the Tao is exactly the same thing as the present moment- that which we call *now* is the same thing as the Tao. The

We do not need to try and solve anything. It is only our false thinking that leads to a false society, which leads to false lives, which leads to false problems. So the attempt to find a solution remains in the false loop and cannot ever succeed to liberate us.

"I have no doctrine to give people,
I just cure ailments and unlock fetters. "
Zen Master Lingi[16]

These 'fetters' that bind us are of our own making. In order to free ourselves, we need only stop making them; which is to say, we must not continue to grasp for any truth whatsoever, or we shall lose the lightness and freedom of the innocent, unknowing mind.

Therefore, God, speaking in Neale Donald Walsch's book, *Friendship With God*, exclaims: "That's been the problem, right there! You've always *thought*. Try *not* thinking once in a while. Try simply *being*. It is when you just 'be'...that the greatest insight comes. ...You cannot find the answer- *any* answer- rapidly by thinking about it. You have to get out of your thoughts, leave your thoughts behind, and move into pure beingness. ...[For] awareness is a state of being. Therefore, if you are perplexed or puzzled about something in life, you must not mind. And when you have a problem, pay it no mind. ...Get *out of your mind*! Remember, you are a human *being*, not a human *minding*. ... [So] you cannot be totally awake while you

---

Tao, the course of things, the eternal now, the presence of God, anything you want to call it- that is *now*! And you cannot get out of it. There is no need to get with it because you cannot get away from it! That is beautiful. You just relax, and you are there." (*The Way of Liberation*, p88)
16 *Zen Essence*, p8

are thinking. Thinking is another form of being in a dream state. Because what you are thinking about is the illusion. ...So every once in a while, it might be good to stop thinking all together. ...Try to avoid labels. ...Just be with the experience. ...Don't look expecting to see something. ...Do not strive to see anything. Relax, and be content with the peace of the emptiness. Empty is good. Creation cannot come except into the void. Enjoy, then, the emptiness. Expect nothing more, want nothing more. ...Let go. Let it be."[17]

Realizing our free and infinite beings is absolutely easy. Effortless even.

As such, in more emphatic verbiage, Helena Blavatsky admonished: "Believe thou not that sitting in dark forests, in proud seclusion and apart from men; believe thou not that life on roots and plants, that thirst assuaged with snow from the great Range- believe thou not, O devotee, that this will lead thee to the goal of the final liberation."[18]

For it is only in surrendered acceptance to the incorrigible enigma that everything becomes wonderful, not in the striving to find an explanation for that enigmaticism.

---

17 *Friendship with God*, pgs. 192-205
18 *The Voice of Silence*, p56. U.G. Krishnamurti- who, like Jiddu, once belonged to the Theosophical society, founded by Blavatsky- offers, in less bombastic terms: "Unless you are free from the desire of all desires, *moksha*, liberation, or self-realization, you will be miserable. The ultimate goal- which society has placed before us- is one that has to go. Until you are free from that desire, you cannot be free from any of your miseries. ...This realization is the essential thing, going as it does to the crux of the problem. It is society that has placed the desire for freedom, the desire for liberation, the desire for God, the desire for *moksha*- that is the desire you must be free from. Then all...other desires fall into their own natural rhythm. You suppress these desires only because you are afraid society will punish you if you act on them, or because you see them as 'obstacles' to your main desire- freedom. ...[That is], any doing in any direction is violence. Any effort is violence. Anything you do with thought to create a peaceful state of mind is using force, and so, is violent. Such an approach is absurd. You are trying to enforce peace through violence. *Yoga*, meditations, prayers, *mantras*, are all violent techniques. The living organism is *very* peaceful; you don't have to do a thing." (*Mind is a Myth*, p46-47)

"Of what significance is meditation when reality is there!"
Jiddu Krishnamurti[19]

Zen Master Huanlong explains: "The Way does not need cultivation- just don't defile it. Zen does not need study- the important thing is stopping the mind. When the mind is stopped there is no rumination. Because it is not cultivated, you walk on the Way at every step. When there is no rumination, there is no world to transcend. Because it is not cultivated, there is no Way to seek."[20]

And Osho similarly maintained: "*Sahaja* [natural] yoga is the most difficult of the yogas, because there is nothing more difficult than to be effortless, natural, and spontaneous ...to flow like air and water, and not to allow the intellect to come in the way of whatever is happening. ...As soon as the intellect comes in the way, as soon as it interferes, we cease to be...natural, and begin to be...unnatural. ...what I am teaching is *sahaja* yoga itself. To impose doctrines and dogmas on life is to pervert life. ...All unnaturalness of our life is this- that we are always trying to be different from what we actually are."[21]

This organic 'Way that is not a Way' is simply about giving up the little discursive machinations that keep us from moving freely and with harmony; by releasing such conceptual constraints we tune into the rhythm of our own beings, right

---

19 *Notebooks*, Aug 1961
20 *Zen Essence*, p19. And yet, given the chronic state of the human mind, Carl Jung pessimistically observed: "People will do anything, no matter how absurd, in order to avoid facing their own souls. They will practice Indian yoga and all its exercises, observe a strict regimen of diet, learn theosophy by heart, or mechanically repeat mystic texts from the literature of the whole world- all because they cannot get on with themselves and have not the slightest faith that anything useful could ever come out of their own souls." (*Memories, Dreams, Reflections*, p175)
21 *Kundalini*, p128,133

ourselves from being 'out of whack', and thus learn to live in the Tao, so to speak.

It is perhaps for this reason that Kerouac wrote: "I wanted to...go off somewhere and find perfect solitude and look into the perfect emptiness of my mind and be completely neutral from any and all ideas. ...to...rest...and do nothing else, practice what the Chinese call 'do-nothing'. I didn't want to have anything to do, really, either with...ideas about society (I figured it would be better just to avoid it altogether, walk around it) or with any...ideas about grasping life..."(brackets are author's)[22]

Effort and knowledge are not required; in fact these are stumbling blocks to the innocent stream which runs through us. We must simply get out of the way. That is the way.

As such, June Singer claimed: "It is only necessary to let ourselves be ourselves. It is not necessary to *learn* how. This may sound like the easiest thing in the world, but for a society that has become expert at manipulating and forcing and conditioning the psyche to function in an adaptive way in a world that appears to require adaptation, there may be much to *unlearn* in the process."[23]

It is this release of the internal corruptions- of every conceptual wall- that allows the real stream of life to rush through.

"At the moment you are most in awe of all there is about life that you don't understand," observed Jane Wagner, "you are closer to understanding it all then at any other time."[24]

---

22 *Dharma Bums*, p105. Chuang Tzu has stated that the wisemen of old "had come to the want of anything that would obstruct the Tao"; which is to say, that through the negation of all that stood in the way of the flow of their true beings- of the heart's movement, of the dance of life- they were 'open', and thus the mystery poured through them, and into them, and swept them away in the flood.
23 *Androgyny*, p273
24 *The Search for Signs of Intelligent Life in the Universe.* Benjamin Tucker wrote: "Too sweet to simply consider elusive, to think it actually needed grasping or understanding, to actually think there was understanding; it was all wonder." (*OF*, p45)

"The ancient Masters didn't try to educate the people,
but kindly taught them how to not-know."
Lao Tzu

The door to infinity forever lies open to anyone who chooses to walk through it. And that door lies within us, and no knowledge, nor action, nor discipline, will help us find it, for it is not by doing or knowing, but by undoing and unknowing that we open ourselves to the truth.

This is an amethodological methodology- the reversal of the mind which is endlessly seeking, for the only way to learn to not-know, is not to 'try' to unknow, but to see knowledge for what it truly is- a hoax; to see that there is no such thing as 'understanding'; in this way we learn to not-know continually.

Ram Dass humbly confessed: "When my guru wanted to compliment me, he called me simple; when he wanted to chide me, he called me clever."[25]

And so the essential re-cognition is that there is nothing to solve, because ...there is no problem; the problem is the search for a solution. For if we use the mind as a way out, we shall be 'way out' but we shall have escaped nothing but ourselves. We must simply acknowledge that there is nowhere to go, there is nothing to do, and there is no knowledge to know. We need only just 'be', and revel intimately in the eternal now mystery of being.

That is, in the relaxed, yet sedulous gaze of honest attention, the natural dissolution of our commonplace self

---

25 It was Ram Dass who coined the 'organic mysticism' axiom of effortless presence- 'Be Here Now!' To 'Be' is to not do. To be 'Here', is to be absolutely present. To be here 'Now', is to have no past and no future, but only what is, and not what is not.

occurs, and though everything remains exactly as it was ...it is no longer commonplace.

"...the attitude of wonder
...is a prerequisite of authentic humanness."
Sam Keen[26]

All is authentic, all is natural, all is mysterious.

Chuang Tzu proffered the following observation: "Knowing enough to stop when one does not know is perfection. ...If a man can understand this, then he may be called the treasure house of heaven. Pour into it and it will never be filled; pour out of it, and it will never be emptied. Yet no one knows why this is so. This is called the hidden light."[27]

Which is to say that to 'stop at mystery' without proceeding 'into' the realm of speculation and therefore hazardously plunging into the realm of context and content, is to remain in the primordial reality, rather than being trapped in the paradigmatic illusion; this is to be consciously ignorant of that towards which one is indeed truly ignorant, and to not flee from this wild and rapturous unknowing.

No matter how sacred or profane, simplistic or complex our models or paradigms of perception and explanation are, they are all nonetheless bound to the limitation of particularization; that is, they are all attempts to explain the parts within the whole, rather than the whole itself (for the word 'analysis', after all, means 'to divide'). And, in fact, these explanations inherently arise from the perspective, capacity, and language of the 'part' itself, which is the individual. Thus, in each case of

26 *Apology for Wonder*, p17
27 *Inner Chapters*, p38

'paradigmatic knowing', the individual merely succeeds to trap him or herself further within the paradigm, by the very act of their own particularized understanding; for they have created a central reference point, a 'knower' within the known, and have therefore limited the limitlessness of the centerless whole.

If, however, there is one and only One Whole, only the whole itself is capable of true understanding and therefore true explanation; the whole is greater than the sum of its parts. Therefore all knowledge- from the linear to the esoteric- is true and valid only within the field to which it belongs, but not as 'truth' *per se*. When a person realizes this completely- that they are only part of the whole- they cease to try to understand from a 'point of view', and instead become softer, less rigid with their definitions of life and of themselves, and in that they merge back innocently into the whole, and the mystery awakens to itself.

Hence Osho proclaimed: "To know is to know that to know is not to know, and that not to know is to know. A real man of understanding knows that he does not know at all. His ignorance is profound. And out of this ignorance arises innocence."[28]

All is marvelous. All is magnificent. All is mystery. We need only be calm and innocent enough, now and forever, to become able to see *It*.[29]

Thus 'true ignorance' is the *sine qua non* for existing within the contextual drama of existence without being helplessly contained by it; ignorance is the ballast of the pilotless and yet unfloundering ship. Upon these waves of awe we need not find a sure anchor, we need only learn how to glide.

---

28 *Ecstasy*, p14
29 Lao Tzu asks: "Can you become enlightened and penetrate everywhere without knowledge?"

"Give up meditation completely and cling to nothing in your mind. You are free in your very nature, so what will you achieve by conceiving?"
Astavakra Gita [30]

It is the fear of the unharnessed mind's boundless infinity- conceptual agoraphobia- that is the plague of our times. Yet it is within our freedom to decide whether we constrain ourselves to the way we have been shown how to know things, or instead choose to open up so as to dream, to breathe in the breath of spirit, and to fall away willingly into the limitless ranges of the possible, regardless of what our confused society has to say about it.

After all, "To stand in awe and wonder is to understand in a very specific way, even if that understanding cannot be described", wrote Gary Zukav. [31]

We must bravely become the destroyers of all our own insecurities and hopes. We ourselves must smash through the walls. For the great paradox of the mind is this: it is not that 'knowing' is the sign of intelligence, but rather it is the knowing of not-knowing; one must be absolutely intelligent in order to witness their ignorance. To be wise is to recognize that one is ignorant; we must be absolutely intelligent in order to understand the profundity of our unknowing. [32]

This recognition would lead Carl Jung to state: "I do not call the man who admits his ignorance an obscurantist; I think it is much rather the man whose consciousness is not sufficiently developed for him to be aware of his ignorance."

And so, "This ignorance", declared Meister Eckhart,

---

30 passage 15.20
31 *The Dancing Wu-Li Masters*
32 The sufi Sina'l stated: "If knowledge does not liberate the self from the self, then ignorance is better than such knowledge." (*Rumi and Sufism*, p24)

"does not come from lack of knowledge but rather it is from knowledge that one may achieve this ignorance."[33]

The more intelligent we become, the more we realize how little we understand. As such we see that adult wonder does not arise from original ignorance, but rather from new ignorance made lucid by the surrender of yesterday's limited knowings; we proceed from denied ignorance, to revealed ignorance.

"The radiant man beckoned me ...he instructed me to isolate myself from conventional thinking and study the wisdom of ignorance."
Richard Moss[34]

The wisdom of ignorance? This is the paradox of paradoxes. And yet it is obvious that knowledge is a failed attempt at emancipating, living, and loving. Thus, after his initiation into mystery, Richard Moss declared: "The wisdom of ignorance: For me it is a sacrament. The acknowledgement of ignorance- that I lack full comprehension of anything- is a sacred act that takes ordinary experience and makes it a door to infinite possibility."[35]

Therefore, claims Osho: "It is always the case that a man of ultimate consciousness and an absolutely ignorant person seem identical- because their behavior is often similar. This is

---

33 And from Haggard we hear, "...the more we learn, shall we not thereby be able only to better compass out our ignorance?" (*SHE*, p251). Thus "Our sense of wonder grows exponentially: the greater the knowledge, the deeper the mystery and the more we seek knowledge to create new mystery", declared Edward O. Wilson, a leading mind behind modern sociobiological research and theory. And Sam Keen stated: "Indeed, for the creative thinker, wonder and humility grow in proportion to knowledge." (*Apology for Wonder*, p34)
34 *The Black Butterfly*
35 *ibid*, p35

why there is always a great similarity between a small child and an old man who has attained enlightenment: they are not actually the same, but, superficially they seem alike. Sometimes an enlightened sage acts in a childlike way; sometimes, in the behavior of a child, we get a glimpse of saintliness. Sometimes an enlightened one looks like an absolutely ignorant person, an absolute fool, and it would seem that no one could be as foolish as he. But the sage has gone beyond knowledge while the child has still to arrive at knowledge. The similarity lies in the fact that they are both outside knowledge."[36]

True wisdom, then, is not so much a profound realization, but a profound unrealization; it is the recognition that true ignorance is not a failure- that perhaps we have simply failed to know what *should* be known- but that such ignorance is instead a success, due to the profound intelligence required to not-know what cannot be known.

> *"You have heard of the knowledge that knows,*
> *but you have never heard of the knowledge that does not*
> *know."*
> Chuang Tzu

'Truth' in the conventional sense is, after all, a terribly uncreative way of acknowledging one's ignorance; knowledge, as it is maintained in the world, is falsely ignorant of true ignorance; it can know everything except one of the most important knowings of all ...mystery. Worldly 'knowing', then, is merely the cowardly not knowing of not-knowing; 'knowing' is unknown unknowing. Which is to say, we are told as children that there is nothing in the darkness that is not there in the light,

---

36 *In Search of Miracles*, p220

but there is one thing- darkness.

Acknowledging this vision of the unseeable, Clarice Lispector wrote: "Perhaps this has been my greatest struggle in life: in order to comprehend my non-intelligence, to understand my feelings, I have been obliged to become intelligent. (Intelligence is necessary in order to understand non-intelligence. Except that the instrument- the intellect- continues to be used from force of habit. And so we are unable to gather things with clean hands directly from the source.)" (brackets are author's)[37]

Let us call this 'The intelligence of ignorance'.

In Dostoyevsky's book, *The Idiot*, Prince Myshkin relates a similar observation, stating: "I may be considered a child even here, but what of that? I am, for some reason, even considered an idiot...but what kind of idiot can I be now, when I realize I'm considered one? When I enter a place, I think to myself, 'They think I'm an idiot, yet I'm intelligent, and they don't realize it-' The thought often occurs to me."[38]

To come upon this type of innocent brilliance we must neither seek to know, nor seek to not know; we must simply ease away and set the contents free; we must not know what seeking is, nor know what knowing is. We must not know 'why?', and we must not know why we do not know why.

"The more you will see, the less you will know.
The less you will know, the more you will yearn.
The more you will yearn, the higher you'll climb."
Dan Fogelberg

---

37 *Jorno do Brasil*, Nov6/71
38 *The Idiot*, p107

And so, we are not moving towards realization, we are moving away; to stop believing things are what we believe they are, we must start again with everything on the table. To go in the mind to where there is no meaning, where nothing connects what we think we are with what we are and what we are not; to sit with neither agenda, nor expectation. This is the unway to try not to come upon a realization.

Aleister Crowley capitalizes his words so as to emphasize the truth of untruth, writing: "KNOW NAUGHT! ALL WAYS ARE LAWFUL TO INNOCENCE. PURE FOLLY IS THE KEY TO INITIATION."[39]

With that key in mind, Iris Dement sings out with lyrical acceptance in her appropriately titled song, *Let the Mystery Be*:

"Everybody is wondering what and where they all came from.
Everybody is worrying about where they're going to go when the whole thing's done.
But no one knows for certain and so it's all the same to me.
I think I'll just let the mystery be."

We must forget the forgettable, become fools, have no purpose, and make the mind new at every moment. We must live without knowing what it is to live, and be without knowing what it is to be. That is how we plug into the mystery. That is how we ...*be*.

"The wise man is he who constantly wonders afresh."
Andre Gide

Thus, "When you have no mind," asserted Master

---

39 *The Book of Thoth*, p253

Dahui, "Zen is easy to find."[40]

And so, Howard Nemerov concludes this section for us with one of his brilliant poetic metaphors, aptly titled *The Way*: "According to our tradition, when a man dies there comes to him the Angel, who says: 'Now I will tell you the secret of life and the meaning of the universe.' One man to whom this happened said: 'Take off, grey Angel. Where were you when I needed you?' Among all the hosts of the dead he is the only one who does not know the secret of life and the meaning of the universe; whence he is held in superstitious veneration by the rest."

*****

---

40 *Zen Essence*, p54

PART II: THE MARRIAGE OF EAST AND WEST[1]

CHAPTER 5: From the Orient

"Before the immensity of mystery one stands like a centipede that feels the ground slipping beneath its feet. Every door that opens leads to a greater void. One must swim like a star in the trackless ocean. One must have the patience of radium buried beneath a Himalayan peak."
　　　Henry Miller[2]

"Sitting there in his plot he was enjoying his own vast emptiness. That way of not understanding was the primeval mystery and he was an inextricable part of it."
　　　Clarice Lispector[3]

"The idea of infinity must have been born on a day of slackening when some vague languor infiltrated into geometry, like the first act of knowledge at the moment when, in the silence of reflexes, a macabre shudder isolated the perception of its object."
　　　E.M. Cioran[4]

"It was an emptiness that had known no knowing..."
　　　Jiddu Krishnamurti[5]

---

1 This section is intended to reveal the similar substratum underlying eastern and western spirituality; that though differing words, ideologies, and actions may appear to be wholly incompatible, when looked at from a certain perspective (or lack of perspective, as it were) there exists, indisputably, a similar profound unreal-ization.
2 *Sexus*, p211
3 *The Apple in the Dark*, p80
4 *A Short History of Decay*, p29
5 *Freedom from the Known*

The Eastern, or Oriental, psyche has seemingly always had a clearer grasp of the subtler metaphysical undercurrents of 'being' as compared with the Occident's more concrete, psychological makeup. And the East has broadcast these realizations in a much more cohesive structure than its western, theistic counterpart; from the Buddha in India, to Lao Tzu in China, to the Zen masters of Japan, there has run a stream of 'detachment' from and 'transcendence' above the conventional, or profane, vision of reality, and this has produced a concomitant distaste for the linear, rational mind.

Thinkers in the East have for the most part considered all that 'is' as 'illusion', and so the ancient masters sought to show therefore that there was no liberation within the context of the illusory world, and thus only by stepping out of (that is, by escaping, or, rising above) the context and recognizing another whole way of seeing things did the individual emancipate him or herself from the limitations society's thought-structures imposed upon life.

This perspective has often, therefore, been divulged through paradoxical and absurd statements about conventional reality, a method that is so patently 'eastern'.

> *"...the still deeper secret of the secret:*
> *The land that is nowhere, that is the true home."*
> The Secret of the Golden Flower

And yet since everywhere is nowhere (now-here), there is no need for one to physically escape life, but instead one can remain in the world while not being tainted by it, for, as Jiddu Krishnamurti pointed out, "...the innocent mind can live in the world which is not innocent."[6]

That is, in a world which is endlessly seeking to belittle the incredible mystery of being through its addiction to facts and 'understandings', an individual can still reverse the process and return to the untainted vision of incomprehension, as we have seen from the last two chapters.

Thus, through the following quotes it can be seen that the mystic East has not simply recommended that one flee the world, escaping into the void, but the masters have instead often suggested that the mystery can and must exist in the cacophony of daily living; one need not seek out esoteric wisdom, or retreat to the monastery, but instead one can come to essential awe through the absence of every idea, understanding, and expectation, while dwelling calmly in the midst of life's myriad 'things'.

It is our false views of the world that lead to our erroneous participation within it. The eastern adepts have therefore realized that the struggle to be released from the sorrow of life comes from the misconception that we are trapped in the sorrow of life; the misconception is conception itself, by which we are 'conceived' into the trap that is not there.

Zen Master Yuanwu asserts, "Once the ground of mind is clarified, there is no obstruction at all- you shed views and interpretations that are based on concepts such as victory and defeat, self and others, right and wrong."[7]

Regarding the 'shedding of views', one method employed in Zen Buddhism, as an attempt to liberate the mind from its conventional fetters, is the *koan*. The purpose of these illogical puzzles- the *koans*- is to strategically disarm the individual's conventional reason, rendering a state of hopeless exasperation, because the *koan*, being a rationally unsolvable,

6 *Freedom from the Known*, p87
7 *Zen Essence*, p28

90

solutionless conundrum, drives the individual into the precarious realm of ambiguous uncertainty- a state which normally the mind, through inveterate tendency, would do anything within its power to deny or avoid, or would invent an answer rather than be left with no answer at all. And so, by the method of the *koan*, the mind is tricked into the inescapable sense and acceptance of absolute non-understanding. An example of a *koan* is the oft quoted "what is the sound of one hand clapping?"

When an individual, struggling with the meaninglessness of one of these problems, finally comes to the state of confounded bewilderment, they have arrived exactly at the place within themselves where they were intended to be all along- they have rediscovered ignorant wondering. Then all that is necessary is to, "Keep that don't-know mind", as suggested by Seung Sahn.

"There is no need to seek Truth; only stop having views."
Seng T'san[8]

For the most part, however, the *koan* is just a trick, and any sedulous, thoroughly honest individual can see that life and its 'purpose' are in themselves the most baffling of riddles; that is, it is almost impossible for an individual not to come to complete, unquestioned incomprehension, by the simple recognition that the mystery of life is unsolvable, incomparable, and everywhere; that life itself is the *koan* of *koans*.

In fact, Zen is so anti-intellectual, that, having been questioned as to why he had chosen Hui-neng to become the sixth patriarch of Zen, Hung-jen, the fifth patriarch answered: "Four hundred and ninety-nine out of my disciples understand

---

8 *Prayer of the Heart*

well what Buddhism is, except Hui-neng." Hui-neng's ignorance was his virtue, because it was the very essential necessary for receiving the highest Buddhist insight. And Hui-neng himself, when asked how he had come to succeed the fifth patriarch, answered: "Because I do not understand Buddhism."[9]

A similar case showing the astonishing requirement necessary for succession along the Buddhist lineage occurred at the very outset of Buddhism when, during his famous Flower Sermon, the Buddha sought to find a successor for his teachings and so had gathered all of his disciples together in one place in order to select one. Standing in front of his entire flock the Buddha simply lifted up a flower without saying anything. Among the hundreds of monks gathered, only one smiled, and he smiled because he did not know what a flower was, and saw only the Mystery to which all mysteries belong, and so he was chosen, and the unbroken chain of 'awakened ones' had begun its acquisition of links.

This feeling of unavoidable incomprehensibility, which precipitates absolute cognitive surrender of its own accord, is one of 'throwing up your hands' in the face of the marvelous ridiculousness of existence, and it is this feeling of flabbergastedness which we must keep always within ourselves, about everything we are, everything we see, and everything we do. To perpetually retain that "don't-know mind", is to dwell in the magical reverie of unknowing, and be liberated from the unmagical mind.

"Let me come to be like a creature without knowledge."
Shen Tao

---

9 excerpted from D.T. Suzuki's *Essays in Zen Buddhism*, p40

To know that ignorance is the pinnacle of real wisdom is to come full-circle within the circumference of the mind; it is to be wise, foolish, oblivious, indifferent and passionate, all at the same time; it is to 'see' everything, and yet know nothing.

Zen Master Xiatang suggests: "Transcend all mental objects, stop all rumination. Don't let either good or bad thoughts enter your thinking, forget all about Buddhism and things of the world. Let go of body and mind, like letting go over a cliff. Be like space, not producing subjective thoughts...or any signs of discrimination."[10]

When we come to that open spaciousness of authentic wonder we must accept it and not allow ourselves to make the mistake of seeking again to find an answer, or a solution to the perplexity, for we must always remember that to formulate any certainty about the mystery which we are, or about why it is unknowable, or the meaning of its meaninglessness, is to return to the forum of the obsolete mind, and to confuse sublime, lucid non-understanding, with vulgar, distorted misunderstanding.

Zen Master Foyan admonished: "Some senior Zen students say they don't rationalize at all, don't calculate and compare at all, don't cling to sound and form, don't rest on defilement and purity. They say the sacred and the profane, delusion and enlightenment, are a single clear emptiness. They say there are no such things in the midst of the great light. They are veiled by the light of wisdom, fixated on wisdom. They are incurable."[11]

---

10 *Zen Essence*, p75

11 *Zen Essence*, p46. Shunryu Suzuki offers a similar observation: "In Japan we have the phrase *shoshin*, which means 'beginner's mind'. The goal of practice is always to keep our beginner's mind. ...In the beginner's mind there are many possibilities; in the experts mind there are few. ...In the beginner's mind there is no thought, "I have attained something." So the most difficult thing is always to keep your beginner's mind. There is no need to have a deep understanding of Zen. ...You should not say "I know what Zen is," or, "I have attained enlightenment." This is the real secret of the arts: always be a beginner. ...It is the secret of Zen practice" (*Zen Mind, Beginner's Mind*, p22)

We must recognize that illusion is *wholly* illusionary; what is absolutely incomprehensible must be left absolutely untouched by the mind, or we may fall into the mistake of believing we 'see' the illusion clearly, and therefore fall further into the mistake that we 'know' that it is an illusion, and why it is such, and how it is going to change, though we really know nothing of it whatsoever.

This is such a difficult threshold to cross that the greatest spirits have never claimed to understand what others claim to understand, and, in fact, they have claimed the exact opposite- they have gone deeper and deeper into complete, humble acceptance of their unknowing.

"My ignorance far exceeds yours."
Shih-t'ou

As such, with great humility, wisdom, and foolishness, Sri Nisargaddata Maharaj admitted: "I do not claim to know what you do not. In fact, I know much less than you do."[12]

The history of true wisdom is, in essence, a lineage of true idiots.

One of the wisest fools of all, Lao Tzu, confessed in the *Tao te Ching*, "I alone have the mind of a fool, and am all muddled and vague. The people are so smart and bright. While I am just dull and confused."

Likewise, although Jack Kerouac was born in the Occident, he was a confirmed student of the East. Mirroring the

---

12 *I AM THAT*, p4. And, as always, with his relentless mortifications, U.G. Krishnamurti announces "From who do you want to know? Not from me. I don't know. If you assume that I know, you are sadly mistaken. I have no way of knowing. ...I myself do not know how I stumbled into this, so how do you expect me to give it to another?" (*Mind is a Myth*, p78,60)

last quote from Lao Tzu, Kerouac concluded: "...everybody, they never listened, they always wanted me to listen to them, *they* knew, I didn't know anything, I was just a dumb young kid and impractical fool who didn't understand the serious significance of this very important, very real world."[13]

So we see, once again, that facts, words, and 'truths' exist only in the realm of the vulgar, and all these categories are but obstructions to the vision of the wise fool. To make a claim of understanding is to prove one has neither understanding, nor ignorance, only pride. Which is to say, in the paradoxical manner of the eastern sages- in order to be thoroughly stupefied by the miracle of our incomprehensible beings, one must be thoroughly, intelligently ...stupid.

***

We now hear briefly from the not-so-distant East- that great land of crazy mysticism, India, where all realms, from the profane, through the symbolic and mythical, to the spiritual and divine, blend into an inexplicable One. In India there has arisen numerous writings containing the same basic realization of human ignorance in the face of the Mystery, and the same admonishment that it is better to accept one's incomprehension and applaud the enigma, than to deny one's ignorance and desecrate it.

> *"Better than the sacrifice of any objects*
> *is the sacrifice of wisdom."*
> Bhagavad Gita

---

13 *Dharma Bums*, p111

To give up expectation, to stop thinking about what one is, or is supposed to do, or what one thinks one knows, and instead to simply 'be'- to forget all about right and wrong, and to dwell in the absence of memory or planning- is to come to exist in the reality of 'what is'. Such is the outcome of the 'sacrifice' of wisdom. From that sacrifice (that is, from surrendering any assumption that one understands life) the now-moment of 'what is' occurs continually to the innocent mind; both the past and future are thwarted from appearing in the individual's thoughts, because the mind is empty of all but the unknowable spectacle dancing in front of the eyes which do nothing but witness the living now. And this miraculous dance of action and repose will not happen...''Till you know and lose this knowing...'', according to the *Mahadeviyakka*. That is, until you sacrifice your 'wisdom'.

The message is clear- we must tangle in the cobwebs of life without being bitten by the spider. We must live in the world of concepts and constructs without falling prey to the limitations which circumscribe them. We must exist within unmystery while yet seeing only mystery.

Lakshminkara called out mightily, "If it confounds you, o seeker, drop concepts now!"

For it is only through the mundane that we come to sense the sacred; they are not two different realms, for there is only One realm. The sacred is the mundane deprived of all its conceptual garments.

As the *Kena Upanishad* states of this One realm: "There the eye goes not, speech goes not, nor the mind. ...Other it is than the known. And moreover above the unknown."

Recognizing this, it is then much easier to give full glory to the magnitude of 'being', surrendering all our pride in knowing, and thus letting life overwhelm us with its remarkable implausibility. Than shall we be wise, for, as the Bhagavad Gita

96

claims: "Wisdom is enveloped in unwisdom, therewith mortals are deluded."

If, then, unwisdom is 'enveloping' wisdom, we must simply get rid of unwisdom; we must clean the slate off completely. Nothing can remain, or the residue will taint what must be pure.

"To know is not to know;
not to know is to know."
Kena Upanishad

We will come to this final, paradoxical recognition only when the linear mind has been completely destroyed. Then the labels we have placed on the seemingly separate parts of the One Whole Mystery will be seen as they truly are- merely labels on fragments of the Great Unknowable.

And then, states the *Kalika Purana*, "You will go wandering about the earth, striking bewilderment into men and women with your flower-bow and shafts, and in this way bring to pass the continuous creation of the world."

*****

CHAPTER 6: From the Occident

Part I: The Fall

"I am sure that in certain quarters the myth will come true, that here and there a link will be found between the unknown men we were and the unknown men we are, that the confusion of the past will be marked by a greater confusion to come, and that it is only the tumult and confusion which is of importance and that we must get down and worship it."
    Henry Miller[1]

"He stood there, stupid, modest, haloed."
    Clarice Lispector[2]

"Here certitudes abound: suppress them, best of all suppress their consequences, and you recover paradise. What is the Fall but the pursuit of a truth and the assurance you have found it, the passion for a dogma, domicile within a dogma?"
    E.M. Cioran[3]

"...religion is not only the graven image in the temple, the letters in the mosque, or the cross in the church, not only the graven image made by the hand, but also the graven image made by the mind, the idea."
    Jiddu Krishnamurti[4]

---

1 *Black Spring*, p191
2 *The Apple in the Dark*, p92
3 *A Short History of Decay*, p4
4 Talks in Bombay, Dec 1958

In the following quotes from the thinkers and mystics of the west it should be apparent that, contrary to popular belief, the religious history of the Occident, specifically that of Christianity, is not simply an unfabulous compendium of categorical dogma, but is, in reality, closely aligned with the more abstract and metaphysical vision of the East, and is, through its own symbols and myths, also an attempt to emancipate individuals from fetters and concepts, to lift us from the Fall, and let the Spirit fly free of its cages.

> *"Thought rises to contemplate its own innerness*
> *until its power of comprehension is annihilated."*
> Kabbala

Firstly then, in order to understand the basis of much of the West's metaphysics, we must go back to the cosmological beginning, where occurred a very important event- mankind's fall from the Heavens. That is, the historic allegory of 'The Fall', which divided mankind from the heavens, occurred for the eating of a very specific variety of fruit- the Fruit of the Tree of the *Knowledge* of Good and Evil. Note, it was not the Fruit of the Tree of the *Doing* of Good and Evil. Thus the 'Fall' was not, as the morally minded priests and theologians would urge us to believe, an ethical event, but was, and is, instead wholly epistemological; that is, in trying to 'know', or claiming to 'know', we divorce ourselves from the Great Unknowable, and then we suffer all the horrors which this unnecessary separation produces in us.

As such, in his book *The Last Temptation of Christ*, Nikos Kazantzakis has Jesus say to a man who is questioning the ways of God: "Don't ask brother: it's a sin. Until a few days ago

99

I too asked. But now I understand. This was the serpent which corrupted the first creatures and made God banish us from Paradise."[5]

The 'fruit' which was eaten is the profane fruition of our separated questionings and understandings, which causes the whole to be divided into fragments, each of which then dwells in the hell of its own separate judging of right and wrong.[6]

Osho states: "This is the meaning behind the biblical story. Adam is turned out of the garden of Eden because he has eaten the fruit of the tree of knowledge. It is a very significant parable. Because of knowledge Adam is turned out of heaven, loses all his blessedness, loses all his innocence, happiness, loses immortality, becomes a mortal, becomes miserable. ...There is no other parable so significant in the whole history of religion. ...Adam's sin is knowledge."[7]

Through the loss of 'innocent looking' we lost unity with the undifferentiated whole, and thus have we come to create a world of opinion, perspective, categorization, and separation. Sin occurs every time that through our separated perspective we think we understand, and through this false understanding and

---

5 *The Last Temptation of Christ*, p116

6 The gravity of this statement will become clearer as the chapters unfold. What is necessary at this point is to realize that Oneness does in fact exist except in the mind which creates division and particularization (i.e. the mind which sees separate events, rather than a contiguous whole). It is the loss of this sense of oneness, called the Fall, which creates our sense of separation from all others, and from the Heavens. And it is this sense of separation which creates our judgement of 'others', for only a separated event can see something as 'other' than itself. Hence the dualistic outlook which projects the perspective of good and evil onto external events is only possible because of the delusionary idea that there are external, or 'separate' events. This is Hell- separation. And therefore any mindset which creates division, in any form, is a mindset which places one in Hell- i.e. outside of Heaven. This is why the very first division- the dividing up of the One into Good and Evil- which then precipitated all other divisions and has created a world of judgement, competition, and separation, is the original cause of our exile from Oneness, and therefore it is the one division which must now be healed in order for our return.

7 *Ecstasy*, p129

judgement about right and wrong we separate ourselves further and further from the Great Unknowable source of ourselves.

It is for this reason, and this reason alone, that we are not allowed to eat from the Tree of Life.

When we have purged ourselves of this ancestral folly, however, we shall return to the Garden through the gate of our knowledgeless Oneness.

"...the 'tree of life', with its fruit of genuine love,
spring[s] up as the 'tree of the knowledge of good and evil'
falls into the ground and dies and is known no more. "
Eom Ida Mingle[8]

Until then we continue to live with the profane vision, of profane things, caused by profane understanding- all because of this 'fall'.[9]

Adam and Eve 'fell' from the space of 'unseparate watching'; they fell into mental separation from the source; for when we particularize what we see, when we seek to label, measure, understand and modify the gratuity of our miraculous beings- because we judge what is 'Good' and what is 'Evil'- that is when we unwittingly set up a false division between the one Source of ourselves, and ourselves; we create a rift between

---

8 *Science of Love with Key to Immortality: The Third Testament*
9 The venerable mythologist, Joseph Campbell, wrote: "Taken as referring not to any geographical scene, but to a landscape of the soul, that Garden of Eden would have to be within us. Yet our conscious minds are unable to enter it and enjoy there the taste of eternal life, since we have already tasted of the knowledge of good and evil. That, in fact, must be the knowledge that has thrown us out of the garden, pitched us away from our own center, so that we now judge things in those terms and experience only good and evil instead of eternal life- which, since the enclosed garden is within us, must already be ours, even though unknown to our conscious personalities. That would seem to be the meaning of the myth when read, not as prehistory, but as referring to man's inward spiritual state." *(Myths to Live By*, p25)

heaven and earth that is not only unnecessary, it is perilous. Judgement, any judgement, is how we separate ourselves from the One. For judgement implies two- right and wrong- and in that duality we lose our singular union. In short, morality is mortality.[10]

It is our cognitive division of the One into the erroneous duality of right and wrong, which exiles us from the eternal union. To return to the Garden then- to regain our innocence- is to stop eating from the Tree of the Knowledge of Good and Evil, and begin again to eat from the Tree of Life; which is to say, it is to lose the mind and the way it separates and particularizes, and instead to open up our hearts and feel the One unknowable life living in and as us. [11]

If we would only live softly, resolute in strangeness, accepting that our limited perspectives cannot do justice to the all, our false way of seeing would cease to shudder through us, and in the movement of that purity all our solemn angst would unavoidably turn to awe.

"The true knowledge and the true vision of what we seek consists precisely in this- in not seeing."
St. Gregory of Nyssa

---

10 A 'channeled' book quotes Jesus as saying: "None really know what the meaning of Pandora's box is until they see that all pain and sorrow were released upon mankind when people began to regard life as an admixture of good and evil." (*Corona Class Lessons*, received by Elizabeth Prophet, p96)

11 Eckhart Tolle offers another view of the same issue; he states: "...when you live in complete acceptance of what is- which is the only sane way to live- there is no 'good' or 'bad' in your life anymore. ...Seen from the perspective of the mind, however, there is good-bad, like-dislike, love-hate. Hence, in the Book of Genesis, it is said that Adam and Eve were no longer allowed to dwell in 'paradise' when they 'ate of the tree of the knowledge of good and evil'." (*The Power of Now*, p150)

Knowledge is, in fact, epistemological blasphemy; we insult the majesty of 'God', so to speak, when we claim, with our little minds, to understand what God is all about. And we return to faith by giving ourselves over to the fact that we exist without knowing how or why- this is when we are 'redeemed' back to the one great mystery itself. And this we accomplish by accomplishing nothing except the annihilation of any separating thoughts or ideas from our minds, and therefore returning again to ignorant innocence.[12]

We can now see that the Occident is not filled to the brim with only orthodox, critical, morally righteous church fathers, casting damnation ruthlessly about towards all transgressors, but there exists also a subtle heritage of more advanced, objective mystics. From them we are shown that we return to the vision of heaven through the destruction of our false vision of earth, for these visions are, in the end, of the same thing- the profane is the sacred; we need only learn to close our corrupted sight off completely, and then to see with innocent, heavenly eyes. Which is to say, we must let what we cannot comprehend remain incomprehensible, that is the only way to give mystery its due. We must no longer eat from the Tree of Knowledge, but now we must gorge ourselves upon the Tree of Unknowledge.[13]

After all, "...this surpassing non-understanding, is 'un-understandably' above every affirmation and denial", as claimed by the anonymous author of *The Cloud of Unknowing*.

This is the way home.

---

12 "The mind of perfect purity is...from the primordial dissociated from good and evil...", claims the non-occidental *kun byed rgyal po 'i mdo* (p161).
13 Recalling Ursula K. LeGuin's description of her book, *She Unnames Them*, quoted earlier, a similar 'redemptive' assertion from Cioran runs: "The fact still remains that our first ancestor left us, for our entire legacy, only the horror of paradise. By giving names to things, he prepared his own Fall and ours. And if we seek a remedy, we must begin by debaptizing the universe, by removing the labels which, assigned to each appearance, isolate it and lends it a simulacrum of meaning." (*The Temptation to Exist*)

What we need is a return to hallowed, intentional ignorance that will lead us out of the darkness of knowing, into the light of the open window of incomprehension.

Meister Eckhart referred to the value of this 'non-understanding', in his exegesis on the first Beatitude, declaring, "...he is poor who knows nothing. ...Therefore we say that a man ought to be empty of his own knowledge, as he was when he did not exist, and let God achieve what he will..."[14]

When knowledge has been exorcised from our brains, we are better equipped to allow the implausible to *be*, and we are more open to realize the inexplicable nature of the universe.

"For in contemplation we know by 'unknowing'."
Thomas Merton

To truly contemplate, is to con-*template*[15]- it is to have a blank slate, no 'template', no image (graven or otherwise), no pattern, no right or wrong, no rules. And from such unconditional openness we regain our birthright in wonder.

Blessed indeed are the poor in spirit, for theirs is the kingdom of mystery.

As Eom Ida Mingle, in her prophetic tome of mystical Christianity, concludes: "...it is in the surrender of both the good and the evil of mortal sense that consciousness of reality of being is identified. ...[For] it is only when the ego has polarized both good and evil in their negative-positive aspects, each being equally non-attractive, that their forces are reduced in consciousness to their primal emptiness, or no-thing, and are

---

14 sermon 28
15 Sam Keen states: "In this regard, contemplation is the effort to evade the tyranny of the already known..." (*Apology for Wonder*, p34)

usable toward reproducing the man of God's idealizing; for the man did eat every tree in the garden, including the 'tree of the knowledge of good and evil,' and died to being, hence, [he] must cease to eat before he can enter into his godly state of being. ...[For] good and evil are unknown in life eternal. ...[Thus] those who have ceased to eat of 'the fruit of the knowledge of good and evil' are eligible to eat from the 'tree of life'."[16]

This 'surrender of *both* good and evil' is quite a task however. The difficulty is professed by Cioran who, seeking support from the east, notes: "In the *Dhammapada* it is suggested that, in order to achieve deliverance, we must be rid of the double yoke of Good and Evil. That Good itself should be one of our fetters we are too spiritually retarded to be able to admit. And so we shall not be delivered."[17]

This is a crucial recognition- that not only must the idea of evil be renounced, but that of good as well, for without one the other cannot exist. To see or seek goodness is to create badness. Thus it is quite a task for ardent optimists and positive thinkers to bridge the gap of good and evil and forge a common

---

16 *Science of Love,* p41,119,139. Similarly, the Native American mystic, Chokecherry Gall Eagle, in his book *Beyond the Lodge of the Sun*, offers a similar perspective, stating: "...the [tree of the knowledge of good and evil] reveals what is good and what is evil. It is knowledge of right and wrong. If everything was created by the Creator and only He existed, then creation came into being as a creation of the Creator's intent. This is the spirit in all things, the Creator within His creation. If everything is perceived as [a] manifestation of the Creator, and imbued with Spirit, there can be no perception of a right or wrong act because everything is within the movements of the Spirit in all things- Holy Spirit. In other words, before eating the fruit, humankind could not perceive right from wrong because everything was within the Holy Spirit in all things, and therefore only good could be perceived. When people ate the Biblical fruit, and could therefore perceive right from wrong, they committed the Original Sin of removing themselves from the flowing Holy Spirit in all things. ...This means that we are not to reach eternal awareness if we can distinguish good from bad. We must return to living in the harmony of Spirit, perceiving only the good and wholeness in Light. If you are in this Garden-of-Eden consciousness, then all your acts are within the flowing motions of the whole, in touch with the Holy Spirit in all things. This is the Grace of God. According to the Bible, we must return to the innocent wonder of childhood with pure hearts." (pg127,151)
17 *The Trouble With Being Born*, p91

one, for to hold onto the hope or idea of the 'good', is to maintain the duality without admitting it, and to still be fallen from the Unknowable, Amoral One.

> **"Ye vainly labour at the rotten kingdom of Good and Evil.**
> **I say that Heaven is Catholic and**
> **none shall enter with susceptibility of either."**
> Austin Osman Spare[18]

Let us note here that, as the original intention of the word 'catholicity' (i.e. open, or broad-mindedness) implies, we must continually advance into, and accept, the vast expanse of our unknowable beings, for the absolute, non-dualistic, living 'isness', or 'suchness', or 'beingness' of being becomes apparent only in the absence of all value judgements.

As such, Frank de Lima, a comedian and ex-catholic deacon, confessed, "I'm very much a product of the church, but sometimes I think my real religion is innocence."[19]

And so, "Out beyond ideas of wrongdoing and rightdoing," wrote Rumi, "there is a field. I'll meet you there. When the soul lies down in that grass, the world is too full to talk about."

The western way, then, is not one of dogma, but one of surrender- absolute, epistemological surrender. Indeed, mystery is the true church within which we unavoidably prostrate in worship of being. We are baptized not in water, but in

---

18 *Anathema of Zos*
19 *Hana Hou* magazine, Apr/May 2000. And Dag Hammarskjold wrote: "God does not die on the day when we cease to believe in a personal deity, but we die on the day when our lives cease to be illumined by the steady radiance, renewed daily, of a wonder, the source of which is beyond all reason." (*Markings*, p56)

disbelief.[20]

This awe-full benediction is pronounced in one of the *Sayings of the Desert Fathers*, which, concluding this section, runs: "Truly Abba, Joseph has found the way, for he said: I do not know."

***

Part II: From the Little Books

We proceed now with supporting quotes from the Bible and its associated apocrypha.

What we find from the words of Western prophets is that, from the outset, they have advised us to travel absolutely naked upon the path back to the Spirit, with neither idea, nor concept, nor understanding of God.

To begin, then, it is arguable that the interpretation of Christ's words regarding how we will know when we have entered the Kingdom of Spirit (that is, "When you take your clothes off, and are not ashamed.") are in reference either to the loss of physical garments around our beings, or to the dissolution of the ego, or to the evaporation of the mental clothes we wear (points can be made for all of these interpretations, and it is likely that all are valid in one way or another, in the shedding of unnecessary traits)- though I would claim the validity of the third interpretation as a supporting analysis for this work (i.e. the shedding of mental clothes leads to the Kingdom of Spirit), for

---

20 Such that Oscar Wilde could claim: "The good Popes hated thought." (*The Soul of Man*, p47)

what we believe we 'know' is but a garment over the 'unknowable'; mystery is hidden behind unmystery. And I would claim corroboration for this interpretation from Thomas Carlyle's book *Sartor Restorus* (or, The Philosophy of Clothes), which, in its vast and eloquent ramblings, expresses largely the sense that it is our mental accoutrements which need discarding if we are to return to Heaven, for "...all Symbols are properly Clothes; ...all forms whereby Spirit manifests itself to sense whether outwardly or in the imagination, are Clothes... [And so] happy [is] he who can look through the Clothes of a Man...into the Man himself...an inscrutable venerable mystery."[21]

Again, 'The Fall' occurs every time we divide ourselves from the unknowable One Mystery (that is, when we clothe ourselves in understanding, thus becoming ashamed of the true nudity of our ignorance) by assuming we understand anything whatsoever of the whole, and especially when we think we understand God.

And so, in attempting to help emancipate us from our mental garments, we are admonished in the second commandment to: "Make not unto thee any graven images..."

And what is a graven image? It is anything that is not fluid, fleeting, and mercurial; any fixed idea, permanent covering, notion, or concept, forming a cognitive wall or filter and inhibiting our perceptual intimacy with the livingness of life.

All images are dead, whether they are in the mind, or carved in stone. Only the spirit which lives without hindrance from preconception or memory is truly alive; the mind, anchored by concept, ceases to be fluid, and 'alive', for it is buried within static thought-structures and therefore has not the plasticity required to engage in the living moment. The supplicant, after all, must be supple.

Thus we must remain like liquid aspects of the whole

---

21 *Sartor Restorus*, p50

(like quicksilver, as it were), without labeling or imagining ourselves as separate, perishable entities. We must see ourselves without the stasis of images- graven images- for these lead to naught but the grave.[22]

To create static images is to divide the living whole into dying particularities. Thus we must be with God and ourselves, without a concept of what we are nor what God is, for if we have an image, any image, we are bound to that finitude and are not free and infinite.

"He who seeks, let him not cease seeking until he finds;
and when he finds he will be troubled,
and if he is troubled he will be amazed..."
Gospel of Thomas

What we are striving to accomplish is a release from the limited context of the manifest, of the flesh, of 'knowing'. We are seeking to return to the freedom and limitlessness of the soul before the fall, when all was divine, mysterious, and mercurial in nature. It is within this living mystery that union occurs between parts no longer seen as separate. That is when mankind and God shall no longer be divided. That is when God is..."Unknown and yet well known." (2 Corinthians 6:9) Unknown because God remains a mystery; known because we are intimate with that mystery.

And that is when "We are fools for Christ's sake..." (1 Corinthians 4:10), as St. Paul advised; to be a fool so as not to be

---

22 Swamiji Shyam offers a unique perspective of this idea: "They are still suffering in any community where the form of God was made. ...It is the form that catches you. When you become 'I am body' of any kind- male or female- you will treat anything else as a form. Then form consciousness, which is called mind, will start functioning and the whole life will be miserable." (Talks, Dec 1998)

divided from the great enigma. For there is one thing we can be certain of- the mind is not the savior, the mind is the trap.

Hence we are admonished that we ought never commit the sin of imagining we 'know', for that only perpetuates the Fall, and does not reunite the whole. As it is stated: "And if anyone thinks that he knows anything, he knows nothing yet as he ought to know." (1 Corinthians 8:2)

This type of castigation is also found in the Old Testament, which contends: "These people, however, revile what they do not understand, while whatever they do know sensually as reasonless brutes, by those things they are destroyed." (Jude 1:10)

It is the reviling of the enigma that is the problem. Therefore we might better understand why the English word 'mystery' is a direct translation from the original Greek word for 'sacred'. For the essential characteristic of the sacred is its secrecy, its mysteriousness.

The unfortunate outcome of the 'Fall', however, is our utter dependence on the mind which makes us 'think we know', and therefore pitifully transforms the secret sacred into the prosaic profane.

To return to the acceptance of not-knowing is to return to ourselves before the fall.

Hence we are beckoned back to God when we are empty of all that is not-God, and if God is Unknowable, then not-God is simply everything known.

"You that are simple, turn in here!
To those without sense...
Come and eat of my bread and wine,
drink of the wine I have mixed."
(Proverb 9:1-5)

110

So it is, that when we have faith (because there is no other option in the face of inexplicable existence), we fall into in awe, for only in that open, catholic, capitulation do we witness the Awesome.

That is when we recognize that "God thunders wondrously...and does great things we cannot comprehend." (Job 37:5)

The banquet is ready, our only duty is to come to it with our most honest hunger; to come without judgement, unfilled and empty, for then shall we be returned innocently to the wondrous delights of the Garden from which we fell.

For, "I am the Lord of good and evil alike." (Isaiah 45:5-6)

And so, "Let him become a fool, that he may become wise." (St. Paul)

For "...God chose the foolish things of the world, that he might put to shame them that are wise..." (I Corinthians 1:27)

Therefore "Stand in awe and sin not..." (Fourth psalm of David)

*****

CHAPTER 7: Immaculate Conception

Part 1: The Virgin

"To become the great lover, the magnetizer and catalyzer, the blinding focus and inspiration of the world, one has to first experience the profound wisdom of being an utter fool."
Henry Miller[1]

"I do not know much. But there are certain advantages in not knowing. Like virgin territory, the mind is free of preconceptions. Everything I do not know forms the greater part of me: This is my largesse. And with this I understand everything. The things I do not know constitute my truth."
Clarice Lispector[2]

"But when we return to ourselves and we are alone- without the company of words- we rediscover the unqualified universe, the pure object, the naked event..."
E.M. Cioran[3]

"The religious man is he who does not belong to any religion, to any nation, to any race, who is inwardly completely alone, in a state of not-knowing."
Jiddu Krishnamurti[4]

1 *Sexus*, p229
2 *Jorno do Brasil*, May6/72
3 *A Short History of Decay*, p121
4 Talks in Ojai, Aug 1955

The image of the 'virgin' has, from antiquity to the present, been a much misused, misinterpreted, and misunderstood aspect of not a few religious mythologies. Therefore, for the intent of this section, instead of engaging in a digressive polemic regarding the truth or untruth of the various schools of thought around the virgin archetype or actuality (the reader might note, however, that currently there are at least the following four definitions of 'virgin' which have been applied religiously: 1: a chaste woman- or man, for that matter 2: an unmarried woman. 3: a self- possessed woman. 4: anyone with a blank or innocent mind), I prefer to cut right to the chase and state that for the purposes of this chapter the reader will come closer to the understanding of the following quotes by recognizing that the definition for 'virgin' which I have accepted is most closely related to number 4, and thus, applied in a more secular sense, is symbolically similar to that which is 'unspoiled or untouched', as in a virgin forest, or virgin country.

Keeping this in mind, it will be easier to make the essential leap that the 'virgin mind' is the innocent and open mind, untrammeled by knowledge and words, and, as it were, without 'conception' (profane conception), and therefore ready to be filled by the Sacred seed.

> *"When it's all over, I want to say: all my life*
> *I was a bride married to amazement."*
> Mary Oliver[1]

Joseph Campbell comments that: "...she is virgin, because her spouse is the Invisible Unknown." For the virgin, in biblical lore, or myth, is the one impregnated by God. And what

---

1 *When Death Comes*

is God, but the Unknowable. Therefore, to be impregnated by the Unknowable, requires the openness of Unknowing. Hence one's conception is immaculate when there is no idea that tarnishes the soul.

"In the mystic world," relates Elisabeth Haich, "the *Virgin* is the human soul which, purged of all earthly dross, has become spotless and has received the divine seed from the spirit of *God*."[2]

Hence it is quite easy to understand the mythological symbology alluded to in the Biblical story where the Virgin Mary becomes impregnated by God without any carnal activity; for carnal activity exists within the realm of particularization, and yet the virgin soul is undivided from the whole, and therefore receives the All without the intermediacy of any part.

Indeed it is the person who is ignorant, and innocent, who is the perfect candidate to receive the spirit. The individual must have a Virgin Mind in order to give birth to the new life.[3]

And what, again, is it to 'be' Virgin? Tom Moore explains: "The virginal psyche is innocent, unknowing, untutored... no simplifications, no adjustments to favored styles of thought and expression, no symbolic shorthand. As in the virginal reflection of dreams, learning and logic have no place in the virginal psyche".[4]

The message should be obvious: The 'virgin mind' (i.e. the unknowing, wondering mind) is the opening through which 'God the Mystery' incarnates into the flesh. Any mind which is not virginal cannot possibly receive the great Unknowable, for such a mind is already filled with limitedness.

Thus the Virgin mind gives immaculate birth to the Child, for "...silence receives as in a womb, the seed of the

---

2 *Initiation*, p248
3 This concept will be better explained in Part 2: The Child, to follow.
4 *Images of the Untouched*, p54

ineffable source," wrote Andrew Harvey, and "... [from] this she brings forth all the emanations of the divine being..."[5]

> *"I must be the Virgin and give birth to God*
> *should I ever be graced divine beatitude."*
> Angelus Silesius

And so, as has been outlined in past chapters, we must continually become absent of 'preconception', by unknowing what we think we know, if we are to be mentally virginal. That is: "To do away with the worshipping of an idol that is an empty ideal, to return back to the virgin self of becoming without any limitations", as Ramtha suggests.[6]

Similarly, describing Mary Magdalene's re-virginization in *The Last Temptation of Christ*, Nikos Kazantzakis wrote: "She had wept and cleansed her soul with tears, had struggled to erase her past from her mind, to forget everything...and to be born again with a virgin body, [then] she felt her soul newly virgin and her lips unkissed."[7]

And later Kazantzakis wrote of the effect produced in Jesus from spending time alone in the desert: "The desert sand was being removed from his body and the virtues and vices of mankind from his soul- leaving it again virgin."[8]

To come to this blessed state of newness, of virginality, we must continually humble ourselves from the false pride of thinking we understand what is right and what is wrong, what is good and what is evil, what is God and what is not-God, thus chastening ourselves until we are chaste of all thought, if we are

---

5 *Son of Man*, p157
6 *Destination Freedom* 1, p38
7 *The Last Temptation of Christ*, p208,209
8 *ibid*, p272

going to continually be virginal, and brides of God. To be virginal is not a one-time event, it is a never-ending openness, allowing the forever-new to continually actualize itself to us.

"Do not know him, for it is impossible; but if by means of an enlightened thought you should know him, be ignorant of him. ...he is united with the ignorance that sees him."
The book of *Allogenes*[9]

It is the continual re-virginization of the mind that perpetuates the living wonder.

Osho describes this necessity as such, "...unless you drop all your knowledge, you will not enter back, you will not be received back. Knowledge is the sin and ignorance is the virtue. ...To be ignorant and to know that all knowledge is false, is a radical revolution. Then you remain virgin. Then knowledge never corrupts you."[10]

Which is to say, we must return at every moment to ignorance, over and over again, and thus eternally be alive to receive the now-mystery of being.

Meister Eckhart reflected on this perspective when he stated: "A virgin, in other words, is a person who is free of irrelevant ideas, as free, as he was before he existed."[11]

So 'virginity' is neither a gender inference, nor a sexual one. It is simply a cloudless sky, a soundless night, or a thoughtless mind. It is the point where the individual re-enters

---

9 from *The Nag Hammadi Library*. And from '*Thunder, Perfect Mind*', another of the codices from *The Nag Hammadi Library*, we have a first-person rendering, which runs: "I am the first and the last. I am the honored and the scorned one. I am the whore, and the holy one. I am the wife and the virgin. ...I am knowledge, and ignorance."
10 *Ecstasy*, p129
11 sermon 24

the pristine womb of beingless being, so as to be born again ...as a child.

***

Part 2: The Child

What is it to be a child? It is to look out at the world and see it as a series of great, dancing, phantasmagorical, kaleidoscopic magical vistas, all of which exist prior to the adult-erated compartmentalization and stultification of the singular, bewildering show.

Sam Keen remarks: "What exactly do we mean when we speak of the wonder of the child? What does the experience look and taste like? Wonder, in the child, is the capacity for sustained and continued delight, marvel, amazement, and enjoyment. It is the capacity of the child to approach the world as if it were a smorgasbord of potential delights, waiting to be tasted. It is the sense of freshness, anticipation, and openness that rules the life of a healthy child. The world is a surprise party, planned just for me, and my one vocation in life is to enjoy it to the fullest- such is the implicit creed of the wondering child. Reality is a gift, a delight, a surprise- in fact, a toy; it is an excessive, superabundant cafeteria of delights, and should any experience begin to be jaded by boredom and staleness, all one has to do is move on to the next. To wonder is to live in the world of novelty rather than law, of delight rather than obligation, and of the present rather than the future."[1]

Aha! What a world indeed. And how odd it is that a child experiences it as he or she does, and adults experience it so differently, and yet it is the *same* world. It seems obvious, therefore, that it is not the world which requires fixing, it is our perspective of it.

It is the child's inherent receptivity to the miraculousness and inexplicability of all that he or she confronts in life that brings the child into direct intimacy with what

---

1 *Apology for Wonder*, p43-44

existence actually is- mystery. And it is the walls of mind which are built up between the growing person and that very Mystery which creates the mental gulf and painful lack of intimacy experienced by adults.[2]

*"This is the rapture of real Being! Innocence is the **inner sense** of the little child, one with the Spirit of God."*[3]

Thomas Traherne's classic description of this observation runs as follows: "Is it not strange that an infant should be heir of the whole world, and see those mysteries which the books of learned men never unfold? ...[As a child] all appeared new, and strange at first, inexpressibly rare and delightful and beautiful. ...The green trees when I first saw them...transported and ravished me, their sweetness and unusual beauty made my heart to leap, and almost mad with ecstasy, they were such strange and wonderful things. The Men! O what venerable and reverend creatures did the aged seem! Immortal Cherubims! And young men glittering and sparkling Angels, and maids strange seraphic pieces of life and beauty. Boys and girls tumbling in the street and playing, were moving Jewels. ...The city seemed to stand in Eden. ...Eternity was manifest in the Light of Day, and something infinite behind everything appeared. ...I knew no churlish properties, nor bounds, nor divisions...so that with much ado I was corrupted, and made to learn the dirty devices of this world. Which now I unlearn, and

---

2 In his book *Dreamgates*, Robert Moss mentions that it is the mind which 'puts the brakes on', and so disallows magic to occur in our lives. He states that, etymologically, the "Greek; *phren*, 'logic', is related to *phrenon*, which means 'brakes'- and 'damper'." (p147)
3 The 'channeled' voice of Jesus received by Elizabeth Prophet, (*Corona Class Lessons*, p97)

become, as it were, a little child again that I may enter into the Kingdom of God."[4]

"For me it is enough to wonder at the secrets."
Albert Einstein

It is likely the case that not all of us have retained such vivid memories of childhood wonder as Traherne, however there seems to be a consistent recognition amongst most of us about the amazingness and freshness which was part of our daily lives as children. We remember at least that to have been a child, was to experience awe.

Similarly to Traherne, Carl Jung relates his experience of infancy: "One memory comes up which is perhaps the earliest of my life. ...I am lying in a pram, in the shadow of a tree. It is a fine, warm summer day, the sky blue, and the golden sunlight darting through the green leaves. The hood of the pram has been left up. I have just awakened to the glorious beauty of the day, and have a sense of indescribable well-being. I see the sun glittering through the leaves and blossoms of the bushes. Everything is wholly wonderful, colorful, and splendid."[5]

Along with Traherne and Jung we can accept that as children we often stood aghast in front of some crazy, mysterious object or happening, like a bug, a flower, or a television, only then to 'grow up' (if I may use this misnomer) and begin to brand these magical happenings with labels, and in the process learn to become ever more and more oblivious to

---

4 *Centuries*, p109
5 *Memories*, p6. Under hypnosis, the writer Whitley Strieber returned to himself as a child, and reports: "I was my childhood self again. It was quite wondrous. ...My mind felt different. Gone was the weight of knowledge. For those few moments, I was innocent again." (*Communion*, p119)

their marvels.

Perhaps this is why Christ stated blatantly, "Unless you become as children, you shall not enter the Kingdom of Heaven." For the Child sees without preconceptions, facts, or theories: the child sees 'what is', and this 'what is', when divorced from our 'fallen' way of seeing it, *is* the Kingdom of Heaven.[6]

> *"The willingness to become as a little child is a primal prelude to spiritual birth, and an essential requisite toward entrance into the kingdom of God. ...This kingdom is attained through repudiating the fallacies of mortal sense based on appearances"*
> Eom Ida Mingle.[7]

Furthermore- entering now into a little bit of esotericism here- the Child, you will recall, is the outcome (that is, comes out) of the immaculate conception. The implication of this is obvious: so as to be 'born again' we must return to what we were (that is, to innocence)- by becoming ignorant, or virginal, of all that is. That is when we give birth to the child within ourselves (we are twice-born).

Eom Ida Mingle, in her heretical orthodoxy, describes

---

6 Sam Keen suggests: "The innocent freshness with which children approach the world has long been held up as an ideal state from which the adult is exiled by the relentless tyranny of passing time. Christianity has suggested that salvation involves becoming like a little child; educators and artists have sought means to awaken in adults the spontaneity, curiosity, and sense of delight that seem to be the rule of childish existence. There is almost universal feeling that some of the patterns of perception which are characteristic of childhood must be recaptured if man is to live an authentic life. Such is the conviction that lies in the back of the association we automatically make between childhood and the state of wonder." (*Apology for Wonder*, p43)
7 *The Science of Love*, p945

this process as such: "...the virginity of consciousness gained is translated into the form and being of the Son. ...[For by] refusing to know the ways of men...the virginal consciousness gained the operation of the Way of God which is Christ. ...Renunciation of the good and evil of mortal sense alone makes for the revealment of the virgin...and lifts man into the Edenic bliss of his divine innocence of consciousness. ...[That is,] the Virgin *in Christ* functions the divine ego and gives birth to himself or herself. ...one puts on the virgin consciousness and is born of the Spirit into the Kingdom of God."[8]

We are dealing here with a little known event, and so the bounds of reason and reasonableness must now be stretched if the new thought is going to exit the womb. What happens in the sublime realm of the spirit is that a person who becomes virginal becomes open to impregnation from the Spirit, and then gives birth. And though the birth is real, it is a spiritual birth, and therefore is not located on the material plane.

> *"...the virgin forever a virgin, forever pregnant,*
> *forever open to possibilities."*
> Marion Woodman[9]

Thus the individual, having become virginal, is impregnated, becoming a mother, and then gives birth, and the child born is also the very same individual. So in one and the same individual is the virgin, mother, and child, and the *pieta* is

---

8 *The Science of Love*, p3,39,267,170,272. And so Stepan Stulginsky suggests that a child is "...virgin of any impression"(*Cosmic Legends of the East*, p119), for the Virgin and the Child occur in one and the same individual. Thus, "I will raise up your son after you, who shall come forth from your body." (2 Sam. 7.12-24)
9 *The Pregnant Virgin*, p7

complete.

This is a truly awkward consideration to grasp, and can neither be proven nor disproven by reason or logic, for it must be experienced.

What happens is a mystical event- a spiritual birth.[10]

Neville comments: "It is a personal mystical experience of the birth of oneself out of one's own skull..."[11]

And Aleister Crowley exalts this two-in-one relationship as such: "I praise the luxuriant Rapture of Innocence, the virile and pantomorphous Ecstasy of All-Fulfillment; I praise the Crowned and Conquering Child whose name is Force and Fire, whose subtlety and strength make sure serenity, whose energy and endurance accomplish The Attainment of The Virgin of the Absolute..."[12]

Again, not only are the Virgin and Child co-substantial, but the Mother and the Child exist inexplicably together as well. Osho describes this contradictory non-duality as such: "...a second birth happens. In this birth you are both- you are the mother and you are the child. You alone are both together. You are born, but there is no separate mother and there is no separate child. You are taking birth, and you are also giving birth; your birth is happening through you."[13]

Hence there is a transformation happening in the individual: becoming virginal of mind brings forth the divine impregnation, creating a mother who births the child.[14]

---

10 Hence Christ stated: "Flesh gives birth to flesh, but spirit gives birth to spirit."

11 *The Law and the Promise*, p147

12 *Thoth*, p122

13 *Kundalini*, p16. Russell Hoban, intuiting this sublime event in his book *Pilgermann*, has Jesus acknowledge that in fact the begetter is the begotten, when he states: "From me came the seed that gave me life." (p27)

14 Note, however, that there is a distinction here- we are dealing with two different occurrences: firstly, the child-like perspective, and secondly, the Child of God birthing. And because it is a tangled affair to denote when these two events are necessarily similar, and where they part, let us only say that to 'become as children' is not necessarily to 'be

This is an event which occurs as the soul evolves and prepares to grow beyond the confines of this material plane. And it is a *real* event, even though it cannot be observed by anyone other than the one to whom it is happening.

This digression on esoteric metaphysics we will have to leave behind, however, and continue on with the theme of the innocent child.

Kahn provides us with a gentle transition back, stating: "The easiest way for the genius [to come to god-consciousness] is to make himself an empty cup, free from pride of learning or conceit of knowledge; to become as innocent as a child, who is ready to learn whatever may be taught to him. It is the soul who becomes as a child before God ...who becomes a fountain of God."[15]

Indeed it is wonder which occurs naturally to and through the child, because the child is not burdened with wonderless knowledge.

"My Guru told me: that child, which is you even now, is your real self. Go back to that state of pure being, where the 'I am' is still in its purity before it got contaminated with 'this I am' or 'that I am'."
Sri Nisargadatta Maharaj[16]

---

born again', for in fact we can return to the innocent mind without necessarily receiving the Spirit into us, although we would expect that, for many cases, one implies the other. However, it is beyond the theological scope of this work to enter into a discussion about the latter event- which is to say, being 'born again' as a 'Child of God'. Suffice it to say that the Spirit chooses the vessel into which it will exist within the manifest, and though the necessity to receive the Spirit is the innocence of the virgin mind, this does not guarantee a divine impregnation- hence, as it is said, "Many are called, but few are chosen."-for there are other factors involved, which, as I have said, are not within the scope of this work.

15 *The Mysticism of Music, Sound, and Word*, p261
16 *I AM THAT*, p239

And so if, as it is said, God is Unknowable, then it is knowledge which prevents one's perception of God the Mystery, and this is why childlike perception is essential, because any perspective which does not see mystery does not see God. Along the lines of this recognition, John Claypool suggests how we arrive at such a place; he states: "This is ecstasy. To be caught up out of one's self in joy over some reality is exactly the sort of experience God wants each one of us to have, for remember we are made in his image, and [this]...is our true destiny. Right here is where the creativity of life is to be found- when we let 'the child within us' out to play and to leap and to celebrate."[17]

To 'become as children', then, is to see everything as new, to fall into wonder, to play in the moment, and to give up the pretense of knowing.

The trick, though, is not to become children again, but to become *like* children; to let go of all grown-up pride and understanding, and to let the magic of existence return.

Osho describes this process about one who has become innocent again; this person, he says, "has come to know that nothing can be known, that knowledge is impossible, that ignorance is the very nature of existence because it is a mystery. In his ignorance he has become relaxed. He rests in his ignorance. He has become innocent like a child."[18]

To 'become as children' merely requires the art of forgetting, for it is only the useless things we have learned which stand between us and the unknowable, and once they are cast aside, nothing remains to obstruct It.

And it is only the Doubting Thomas within us which cannot accept the possibility of a return to mind boggling wonder- as it was with the disciple who doubted that it was

17 *The Light*, p135
18 *Ecstasy*, p149

possible to be reborn again, to enter into the womb for a second time. And yet that is the very problem: trying to conceive of the inconceivable, which is a vicious circle from which there is no escape. The mind creates the walls, and the mind defends them, and it is only after the hubris of thought has dwindled to nothing that the soul becomes youthful again.

> *"A child said What is the grass?*
> *fetching it to me with full hands;*
> *How could I answer the child?*
> *I do not know what it is*
> *any more than he."*
> Walt Whitman[19]

Speaking of his youthful inwardness, the well-humbled Prince Myshkin (from Dostoyevsky's *The Idiot*) unabashedly declared: "[My doctor]...was quite convinced I was an absolute child, that is to say, I resembled a grown-up only in stature and face; in development, spirit and nature, and perhaps even in mind, I was not an adult at all, and would remain that way even if I lived to be sixty."[20]

To come to this place of innocence, like Myshkin, we must relinquish all sense of propriety, responsibility, accomplishment, knowledge, success, honor, and need. We must return to the unquestioned trust of a child in the midst of all things magical, for: "When you become the rigid, unyielding adult who is lost to the ability to embrace the imaginative and non-judgemental nature of the child within, then you become lost to the sense of wonder and playfulness that you are intended to

---

19 *Song of Myself*
20 *The Idiot*, p106

experience", states a 'channeled' version of Jesus' teachings.[21]

To become new of mind at every moment, is to forget all we have learned, and to begin to see the world as if for the very first time; unless we do this we are doomed to continue to see life in the profane, linear, fragmented and fragmenting way we have been taught, and never to see it as the brilliant, spirited, genuine drama of the free and unknowable Spirit to which we entirely belong.

And so, the door to heavenly wonder can only be opened, contends Pila Chiles, with "A key that can only be turned by the child. ...One who has had the courage to embrace innocence again and regain the power, the childlike wonderment. ...This is the innocence that explores the world...bringing back the joy which is the pure excitement of living in our Maker's creation."[22]

"The more you know, the more you feel how ignorant you are.
And those who are really wise, they become ignorant.
They become as simple as children or as simple as idiots."
Osho[23]

Let us end this chapter with Oscar Wilde's splendid proclamation of the necessity of our regressional evolution. He

---

21 *The Wholly Bible*, p63
22 *The Secrets and Mysteries of Hawaii*, p206. White Eagle writes: "... we are touching on a very great mystery, just catching a glimpse something that really must be felt to be understood- and before which we are surely all as children. ... [So] to become as little children means that there must be a transference from thinking in the brain to feeling and intuition in the heart center." (*Jesus, Teacher and Healer*, p92)
23 *The Book of Secrets*. Providing an example, Osho states of the infamous Indian poetess: "Lalla lived naked... In her nudity people saw for the first time a beauty and innocence that were simply extraordinary. She radiated the innocence and joy of a child." (*Kundalini*, p123)

states: "It will be a marvelous thing- the true personality of man-when we see it. It will grow naturally and simply, flowerlike, or as a tree grows. It will not be at discord. It will never argue or dispute. It will not prove things. It will know everything. And yet it will not busy itself about knowledge. It will have wisdom. ...The personality of man will be very wonderful. It will be as wonderful as the personality of a child."[24]

*****

---

24 *The Soul of Man*, p27

PART III:
THE WHOLE AND THE BROKEN

CHAPTER 8: Necessary Newness

"Abandoning the cunning instruments of the mind with which he had vainly hoped to pierce the mystery, he now stands before the veil of creation naked and awe-struck. He divines what is in store for him. Everything becomes personal in a new sense. He becomes himself a new person."

    Henry Miller[1]

"All sudden understanding is in the last analysis the revelation of a clear nonunderstanding."

    Clarice Lispector[2]

"One touch of clearsightedness reduces us to our primal state: nakedness..."

    E.M. Cioran[3]

"That is, can I die to each action throughout the day, so that the mind never accumulates and is therefore never contaminated by the past, but is always new, fresh, innocent?"

    Jiddu Krishnamurti[4]

---

1 *Wisdom of the Heart*, p172
2 *The PASSION according to G.H.*
3 *A Short History of Decay*, p14
4 Talks at Saanen, Aug 1964

In keeping with the theme of the last chapter, it is easy to recognize that the salient factor of the child's innocent perception is that everything appears continually new; in newness there is no moment but 'now', there is no memory of what life was, nor knowledge of what one *is*, nor expectation of what will follow; life is a continuum of unique, novel, inexplicable experiences.

This sense of ever occurring newness is one of the hallmarks of approaching the benediction of wonder, for it is through ahistorical vision that we see life as if for the very first time and come to recognize its profound, unbelievable implausibility. And this perception of newness comes to the child without effort, for the child does nothing but perceive 'what is' without memory, and that alone makes 'what is' perpetually new.

> *"[Life]...doesn't need understanding. It needs newness."*
> D.H. Lawrence[5]

The living moment is always now, always new, and always ending and beginning. We simply fail to recognize this because we are too lazy to pay attention, too lazy to forget, too lazy to "care for the watching", as Jiddu Krishnamurti continually admonished. Yet when our living consciousness is freed from the Form, it cannot help but despise stagnation and repetition. Just as a spectator would prefer to watch a new episode of an ongoing television show, rather than a repeat performance, so it is with the innocent, 'detached' witness, who seeks not the security of 'what has been', but instead seeks newness always, if for no reason other than the joy of novelty.

---

5 *The Man Who Died*, p76

And so, if we are to come to the self-effacement necessary to truly embrace the ever-unfolding newness of *being*- to lose ourselves at every moment, and live as if for the very first time (a fact which is easy to rationally understand, but extremely difficult- or devilishly easy- to assimilate into our conditioned perceptions)- we must learn to see the beauty and magic eternally occurring new at every moment ...which never was before. *We* must be new at every moment.

Now, with the term 'self-effacement', as used in the above paragraph, I have encroached dangerously into the problematic topic of 'psychological surrender' (as opposed to 'epistemological surrender'). However, it appears that both of these capitulations are so inextricably interconnected, that if we attempt to tackle one, we must necessarily end in dealing with both.

The moment you do not know who or what you are, the ego dissipates, and all vanity and neurosis melt away along with it. Incomprehension is the least painful way to die, to lose everything you thought you had, to become as nothing, and to be born again always new from the ashes. Thus the phoenix, so often used in alchemical symbolism, represents the new person rising out of the death of the old.

"I simply don't know. In fact, I sometimes think I am not me.
I seem to belong to a remote planet,
I am such a stranger unto myself."
Clarice Lispector[6]

Yet this is perhaps the most problematic item to erase in the act of forgetting- oneself. How to be oneself, and yet forget

6 *The Hour of the Star*, p36

oneself? How to turn one's vision inward, and then with a dexterous maneuver, choose to go blind? It is a sublime and effortless event, for now it is not simply the known which must be forgotten, now it is also the knower.

Regarding this topic, Osho relates: "When you don't know, you are not. When you know, you are. Knowledge begins to function as the ego. No-knowledge, and the ego cannot exist; it has no props, no support. It falls, collapses, and disappears. And in that state of no-mind, no-ego- no-you- something happens which is more like love. You flow into existence and existence starts flowing into you. You are no longer separate from the existence. The drop has fallen into the ocean, and the ocean into the drop. ...New centers will be awakened, a new individuality will emerge, new experiences will happen-everything will be new. If you are prepared for the new then you must gather courage to part with the old. ...We have to destroy the old man and its ugliness, its rotten ideologies, its stupid discriminations and idiotic superstitions, and create a new man with fresh eyes, with new values- a discontinuity with the past."[7]

To forget ourselves is simply a matter of forgetting our knowledge or understanding of ourselves. It is to allow that we are perhaps something very different than we have ever imagined; that perhaps we should not be confining ourselves within the limitations of the mind, and that therefore the essential thing is to divorce ourselves from any image, description, or characteristic. The essential thing is to set ourselves free.

Richard Moss offers the same message, albeit in different terms, writing: "Before we define our experiences, before we accept the labels of our conditioned thoughts and

---

7 *Ecstasy*, p130, *Kundalini*, p12. This perspective is summed up by U.G. Krishnamurti, who offers: "Your knowledge coming to an end means that *you* are coming to an end." (*Mind is a Myth*, p45) And, from a lateral angle, Eckhart Tolle claims: "So the single most vital step on your journey toward enlightenment is this: to learn to disidentify from your mind." (*The Power of Now*, p17)

feelings, we must learn to create a space of unknowing- a space of openness to new interpretations."[8]

And that space we create must never be filled, it must always be purged, like a conduit, with life flowing, and never stopping, through it; we must make the mind new, not once, but at every moment. We must forget ourselves not once, but always, if the ever new is to occur continually both inwardly and out.

"Out of this emptiness the new is."
J. Krishnamurti[9]

The path is one of continual negation, not one of insatiable accumulation; reason must vanish altogether, taking with it both memory and conditioning- if we are to look out at a world we have been living in all the while, and look into a self we have been calling 'I' for the same amount of time, and in the living instant suddenly unknow everything completely and see life as if we have never ever seen it before.[10]

J. Krishnamurti suggests: "...the moment you have a conclusion or start examining from knowledge you are finished, for then you are translating every living thing in terms of the old. Whereas if you have no foothold, if there is no certainty, no achievement, there is freedom to look, to achieve. And when you look with freedom it is always new. A confident man is a dead human being."[11]

---

8 *The Black Butterfly*, p3
9 *Freedom from the Known*
10 Upon the bathtub of King Tching-thang was inscribed the axiom: "Renew thyself completely each day; do it again, and again, and forever again."
11 *Freedom from the Known*, p25. Similarly, Nicholas Roerich declared, "We cannot give statements of finality because each finality is a conclusion, and conclusions mean

133

To reach the spontaneity of living nowness is incredibly subtle. Joseph Chilton Pearce describes this adaptation to existence as a "...casual, haphazard, amoral process that leaps the logical gaps and brings about newness."

This statement is a spectacular, parsimonious synopsis of the way of unknowing: to be 'casual' is to be without 'living by the letter'; to be 'haphazard' implies a conditionless event; and 'amorality' is the absence of the Fruit of the Tree of the Knowledge of Good and Evil; all of these traits- casual, haphazard, and amoral- then conspire to bring the individual to the realization of newness (of witnessing creation continually creating).

In our pursuit of wholeness, it is not a debt to old wisdom which we owe, but a new ignorance which we must inherit. It is not the meaning, but the mystery of being which we must re-dis-cover. Our new truths should not demystify the world, they should remystify it.

> *"Since I scoured my mind and my body,*
> *I too, Lalla, am new, each moment new."*
> Lalla

This is the way to be 'born again', as we have seen- to be new again, and again, and again. Hence Augustine's injunction to "Be reformed in the newness of your mind."

It is this 'new mind' which Christ referred to in the gospels, and which was translated from Aramaic into the Greek word, '*metanoia*', which means, in English: a 'change of knowing' (*meta:* change; *-noia:* knowledge), or 'to know differently than you now know'. This word, *metanoia*, which is

---

death." (*Shambhala*, p221)

absolutely epistemological in its root and essence, has been disastrously mistranslated in the English Bible as the morally burdened word 'repent'. Yet even re-*pent* (as in *penser:* to think (Fr.)) has the historical quality of a reversal of the mind. Thus we see that Christ was not an ardent moralist, bent on exacting merciless penance from recalcitrant sinners, but was instead attempting to bring about a new mind by radically shifting the individual's consciousness away from the erroneous outlook of the day. [12]

And why must we 'change' (i.e. re-pent) the way we see things? Because we shall not see the 'new' until we stop seeing the 'old'. We shall not begin to see clearly, until we cease to see unclearly, until we have a '*metanoia*'.[13]

The lessons of the occident are clear: we must not create graven images, but instead become as children by repenting of our old ways of thinking, therefore entering with virgin minds into mysterious newness.

But what that newness is we certainly cannot suppose, for that supposition would be based on the old mind, and therefore the only option is to relinquish 'what was' and create a space for what 'will be'. This statement is explained by Stepan Stulginsky, who states: "It is dreadful when people approach new conditions with their old habits. ...Only the blind can think that tomorrow will be like yesterday! The world in confusion demands the search for new ways. The aspiration of humanity toward the unusual will give it the understanding of the New. ...[But] before the rise of the New...the old foundations crumble.

---

12 I turn for support on this exegesis to a true authority on the subject: "New thought is your only chance. It's your only real opportunity to evolve, to grow, to truly become Who You Really Are. Your mind is right now filled with old thoughts. Not only old thoughts, but mostly someone else's old thoughts. It's important now, it's time now, to *change your mind* about some things. This is what evolution is all about." God (*Conversations with God*, by Neale Donald Walsch, p168)

13 "No man putteth new wine into old skins..." (Mark 2:22). "Behold, I make all things new." (Rev 2:15)

Thus, upon the ruins of [our] old world there rises a new evolution."[14]

As above, so below. As without, so within.

"Old things are past away, all's become new.
Strange! He's another man, upon my word..."
John Bunyan[15]

This idea of renewal is expressed in more contemporary terms in Thomas Kuhn's landmark work *The Structure of Scientific Revolutions*, where, supplying numerous examples from the history of science, he emphatically argues that scientific revolutions do not come about from the discovery of new data, but from the ability to see the old data in a new way. The new 'paradigm' is simply a different way of visioning the old observations. Thus, scientific revolutions come about most often from younger, newer arrivals into the scientific fields- from individuals who have not yet had the openness and creativity of their minds thwarted by being compelled to look at things continually in one way, and one way only (i.e. the current paradigm). Therefore the revolutions come about because the new-breed can see things differently than the conditioned, old-school sight of their predecessors.

Paradigms must crumble regularly, as the ever-new takes the place of the ever-old.

Hence Herbert Guenther suggests: "This 'sense' may be said to be the feeling of wonderment, not so much as a passive state, but as an active, and, in the strict sense of the word, a creative manner of looking at our familiar world, as if it were for

---

14 *Cosmic Legends of the East*, p125
15 *Pilgrim's Progress*

the first time."[16]

Here we have a way of seeing the ever novel, dynamic manifestation of life- by obliterating our vision from its conditioned stasis, and viewing it through different eyes. To see and be new, we ourselves must become emptied of the old, that is all. An internal renaissance must occur. Startlement is the starting point, from which one becomes 'dumb-founded'.

Again, to see with new eyes we must unthink with new minds, now and at every moment, or we shall see nothing more than what we wrongfully saw the moment just before.

Which is to say, newness *is* wonder.

Now it is possible to understand that the term 'original mind', as propounded largely by the oriental mystics, does not refer specifically to the finding of a particular frame of mind and then dwelling forever within that way of seeing, but instead it is the continual, moment to moment, return to the origin, to the ever unconditioned, dynamic, eternally creative newness that lies eternally within all of us. This is our surest way back to awe.

"When you see *there are no longer familiar features in the world. Everything is new. Everything never happened before. The world is incredible!"*
Don Juan

In fact, all we need to do is recognize that we do not understand at least one thing which we thought we understood, and subsequently every other thing related to it then becomes suspect, and we may suddenly look upon a world which we have never truly seen before. The most commonplace occurrence can

---

16 This is an editorial comment by Guenther in his translation of *Kindly Bent to Ease Us*, by Longchenpa.

be the catalyst to seeing fresh novelty everywhere.

Martin Heidegger stated: "In wonder what is most usual of all and in all, in whatever manner this might be, becomes the most unusual."

How could it be otherwise? Until we recognize that we do not understand what we thought we understood- which is everything- we shall not stand in dutiful reverence to the nonunderstandable, and we shall not look at ourselves nor the world in any way other than the way we have been shown.

Wisdom is the living Sophia, so long forgotten in the playless rules of philo-sophia.

The Dadaist, Georges de Chirico claims: "Above all, what we have to do is to rid art of everything it has known until the present, every subject, every idea, every thought, every symbol has to be tossed aside. ...Only when our thinking has been cleared of all that we call logic and sense, when it has removed all its human shackles, will things appear to us in a new light as though illuminated by a constellation that has appeared for the first time."[17]

---

17 This quote now ties together some early descriptions of the way of the true artist: from Miller: "...a writer...ramified the mysteries, extended them, developed them, and left the answers to go hang..."(from The Myth of Knowing), and Nietzsche: "...as artists we are learning to forget and not know"(from the Art of Forgetting). What we find from these observations is that art is largely about newness: hence the name for one of the most popular forms of art, the 'novel', is a *double entendre,* meaning also, of course, a 'unique event' (i.e. novel occurrence) in the cosmos; hence the origin of the word 'poetry', which is *poesis,* also means 'creation'; hence even the word 'art' (which we have evolved to use as a noun), is derived from the verb 'art' (as in, "...where for art thou?", or, "...who art in Heaven." etc.), and in this sense is a term used synonymously with 'will', and therefore implies action and not stasis. So we begin to see that the definition of art, or creation, necessarily implies living newness. To be an artist is to create that which has not yet been, otherwise it is merely re-creation, or plagiarism. Oscar Wilde summarizes this beautifully, stating: "[Art]...seeks to disturb...monotony of type, slavery of custom, tyranny of habit, and the reduction of man to the level of a machine. ...the artist...has made a beautiful thing that is new...[such that] an educated person's ideas of Art are drawn naturally from what Art has been, whereas the new work of art is beautiful by being what Art has never been; and to measure it by the standard of the past is to measure it by a standard on the rejection of which its real perfection depends. A temperament

This observation carries over into all of life. Creation creates. Everything that is taking place now and always is eternally new. Life is art. There is nothing but newness always happening.

Now, taking a giant leap forward, if we recognize that all of life is Creation- if all of life is art- then *we* ourselves are art; we are what is eternally new at every moment. We must not only see the world again from a novel standpoint, we must also learn to see ourselves, our 'I', as if we had never known ourselves before. And this we must do not just once, but always. The 'I' that is in all of us must never become old, but instead must be renewed over and over again with the passion of forgetful wonderment.

"You fear so much to become ridiculous... And you are shocked at the call: Be new! be new! Not as on a stage, but in your own life."
Nicholas Roerich[18]

Hopefully this never-ending process will eventually cause all of us to imperfectly exclaim, along with Robert Graves, "I in a new understanding of my confusion", and with Russell Hoban's unlettered, vernacular character, Riddley Walker, "Right then I dint know where I wer with any thing becaws all on a suddn I wernt seeing any thing from where I seen it befor."[19]

For if we do not wipe the knowledge of ourselves- the belief that we do, or can, understand ourselves- from the very

---

capable of receiving...new and beautiful impressions, is the only temperament that can appreciate a work of art." (*The Soul of Man*, p36,37,44)
18 *Shambhala*, p153
19 *Riddley Walker*, p96

fabric of our lives, we will not reach our exalted selves, but instead we will continue to believe that we are not the mystery which we are, and so continue to live how we shouldn't.

When the true, new ecstatic opening occurs in the mind- when the ground breaks out from beneath us and leads to absolute aghastness, and to basking in the fabulous glow of never-ending novel wonder- this is simply the most enjoyable of all possible vertiginous apocalypses.

Yeats suggests, "In the Purification...new...takes place of the old; made from the old, yet, as it were, pure. All memory has vanished, the Spirit no longer knows what its name has been, it is at last free in relation to Spirits free like itself."[20]

Truly this is to be intimate and yet alien with all that is. And so, contrary to the assertions of academicians, logicians, and pedants, it is the event which nonplusses us which is more essential than the one which expounds; true 'realization' is not the dissolution of enigma, but the exposure.

"The real act of discovery consists not in finding new lands but in seeing with new eyes."
Marcel Proust

Once again, in order to start back at square one, without a hint or clue about what we are, why we are, or where we are going, we must not seek to find something, we must seek only to lose everything. And what remains, after all the dross of the mind is cleared away, is the fresh witnessing of the living, unfathomable spirit, which we will never see until we have stopped seeing the world and ourselves the way we have been shown to see these all along, which is to say- falsely. We must

---

20 *A Vision*, p233

exorcise the old, before we shall give birth to the forever new.

> *"To re-create yourself anew always...*
> *this is the purpose of life."*
> God[21]

*****

21 *Conversations with God III* , by Neale Donald Walsch. "But now we have been delivered from the law, having died to what we were held by, so that we should serve in the newness of the Spirit and not in the oldness of the letter." (Romans 7:6)

CHAPTER 9: Death and Resurrection

"The disorientation and reorientation which comes with the initiation into any mystery is the most wonderful experience which it is possible to have. Everything which the brain has labored for a lifetime to assimilate, categorize and synthesize has to be taken apart and reordered. Moving day for the soul!"
Henry Miller[1]

"Because having touched upon the incomprehensible knot of the dream he accepted the great absurdity that mystery is salvation."
Clarice Lispector[2]

"...This is the hernia of image, the transcendental rupture of poor words, born of everyday use and miraculously raised to the heart's altitudes."
E.M. Cioran[3]

"You cannot live without dying. You cannot live if you don't die psychologically every minute. This is not an intellectual paradox. To live completely, wholly, every day as if it were a new loveliness, there must be a dying to everything of yesterday, otherwise you live mechanically, and a mechanical mind can never know what love is or what freedom is. ...To die is to have a mind that is completely empty of itself, empty of all its daily longings, pleasures and agonies. Death is a renewal, a mutation, in which thought does not function at all because thought is old. When there is death there is something totally new. Freedom from the known is death, and then you are living."
Jiddu Krishnamurti[4]

---

1 *Tropic of Capricorn*, p220
2 *The Apple in the Dark*, p237
3 *A Short History of Decay*, p65
4 *Freedom from the Known*, p77-78

Having recognized the absolute necessity for the mind to die from its old ideas and preconceptions, so as to make room for the eternally new, we will now examine the process by which an individual undergoes such a cognitive death and resurrection.

For every action there is an equal and opposite reaction, and this statement applies as much to metaphysics as it does to physics. Having been lifted into the stratosphere of exaltation on the wings of awe, not a few individuals find themselves returning to the world with all the grace of Icarus. This is because the experience of absolute wonder destroys false walls, and does not create new ones; everything false is demolished, and nothing but the real, stupefying nudity of 'what is' remains. For the most part, this rapture is a positive experience, but because everything a person 'understood' is suddenly and thoroughly disproven, many individuals coming to this 'unrealization' cannot endure the expansive infinity confronting them, and so tumble down from that great height.

"We ought to dance with rapture that we should be alive and in the flesh, and part of the living, incarnate cosmos."
D.H. Lawrence[1]

We ought to be mad with disbelief, aghast with awe, engrossed with gratitude, and joyful with incertitude. This is how we should be, but this is not how we are.

At the threshold where the cacophony of the limited mind drops away, many individuals find themselves in a debilitating whirlwind of exasperation, making it impossible to take a firm grip upon conventional existence again, and therefore causing them to drift helplessly off into the fringe realms of life.

---

1 *Apocalypse*

This sounds bleak, and perhaps it is, but, as the saying goes, "the road to heaven leads through hell."

When the limited, programmed mind finally opens up to the infinity of the mystery which has been repressed until then, a person often finds him or herself drowning in limitless implausibility, and this does not assist the individual to lead a responsible, capable, limited life. For when the mind is finally divorced from all its previous assumptions, ideas, and understandings, it suddenly stands upon the brink of the chilling Unknowable. It is at this point where some sink, some swim, some fall to their deaths, and some ...learn to fly.

This is the vertiginous uncertainty of life, of absolute incomprehension, when all supports and suppositions come crashing inexorably to the ground. There is nothing left to grab hold of. The slate is wiped clean, and because you yourself are also on the slate- you are gone as well. This may sound extreme, but that is because ...it is extreme. I am speaking of an inner Apocalypse, a death which goes either nowhere, or ...leads to further life.[2] The individual who undergoes such a catastrophic and transforming undoing cannot continue living with the conceptions of life he or she had previously existed within. That is the beauty and horror of wonder.

*"...the whole terrain founders, the soil underfoot is afloat,
the constellations are shaken loose from their moorings,
the whole known universe, including the imperishable self,
starts moving silently, ominously, shudderingly serene
and unconcerned, toward an unknown, unseen destination."*
Henry Miller[3]

---

2 David Icke observes: "The real meaning of apocalypse, as I understand it, is the 'revealing', the 'unveiling'." (*Lifting the Veil*, p135)
3 *Tropic of Capricorn*, p207

And it is exactly this dis-*solution*, which is the initial requirement for rapture.

A short synopsis of what happens is this: we are born, and grow up, and go to school, and learn to read and write, and to 'know' things, and so we proceed through our days without the slightest inclination that everything we believe to be true is merely opinion, excuse, or misinterpretation; that we have defrauded the grandiosity of being by conceptualizing within the context of limitedness; that we have persisted in the shallows of interpretation and learning, only because of a habitual fear of the height of awe. And when finally we realize that all we have come to 'know' and believe as reasonable explanations for life are but confused make-shift veneers hiding all that is truly incomprehensible, the whole show comes tumbling down.

A brief anecdote from Jouffrey will help to explain: "I shall never forget that night of September in which the veil that concealed from me my own incredulity was torn. I hear again my steps in the narrow, naked chamber where, long after the hour of sleep had come, I had the habit of walking up and down. ...Anxiously I followed my thoughts as they descended from layer to layer towards the foundation of my consciousness, scattering one by one all the illusions that until then had screened its windings from my view, making them at every moment more clearly visible. Vainly I clung to these last beliefs as a shipwrecked sailor clings to the fragments of his vessel, vainly, frightened at the unknown void into which I was about to float. I turned with them towards my childhood, my family, my country, all that was dear and sacred to me; the inflexible current of my thought was too strong- parents, family, memory, beliefs- it forced me to let go of everything. The investigation went on more obstinate and more severe as it drew near its term, and it did not stop until the end was reached. I knew then that in the

145

depth of my mind, nothing was left that stood erect. ...This moment was a frightful one, and when, towards morning, I threw myself exhausted on my bed, I seemed to feel my earlier life, so smiling and so full, go out like a fire, and before me another life opened, somber and unpeopled, where in future I must live alone, alone with my fatal thought that had exiled me there, and which I was tempted to curse. The days that followed were the saddest days of my life."[4]

From Jouffrey's confession it can be seen that despite the undeniably exhilarating effect of absolute non-understanding, there is often a negative reaction, a terror, at the collapse of all cognitive grounding.

"It seams like every body elses got ansers
only I haven't got nothing only askings."
the colloquial Riddley Walker[5]

This 'conceptual agoraphobia', as it were, can be the undoing of the individual who is blessed with the privilege of complete wonder; the negative response often leads to the pathos of the 'outsider', driving him or her into loneliness and insanity. This type of response is a large thread woven through Colin Wilson's brilliantly written work, *The Outsider*, from which Jouffrey's quote was taken. In his exhaustive study of individuals on the crest of consciousness, Wilson shows how anyone who divorces themselves from the meanings imposed upon life by mankind no longer fits anywhere into a society whose truths are seen to be completely false. This leads, in his book, to a thesis on tragic individuals who, for the most part,

---

4 quoted in Colin Wilson's book, *The Outsider*
5 *Riddley Walker*, by Russell Hoban, p171

have fallen away from the world of men, because they have seen 'too deeply'.[6]

Colin Wilson explains the general nature of the outsider's predicament, by saying, "Without the meaning his Will would normally impose on it, his existence is absurd."[7] Wilson then gives, as an example of that absurdity, a quote from H.G Wells, who stated: "Hitherto, events had been held together by a certain logical consistency, as the heavenly bodies have been held together by gravitation. Now it is as if that cord had vanished, and everything was driving anyhow to anywhere at a steadily increasing velocity... A harsh queerness is coming into things... We pass into the harsh glare of incredible novelty. ...The more strenuous the analysis, the more inescapable the sense of

---

6 This predicament reminds me of J.D. Salinger's societally frustrated, or inept, characters brought to life in his marvelous works. I am thinking specifically of Holden Caulfield in *The Catcher in the Rye*, who, at a very young age, could see the 'phoniness' in people and all life, and therefore became a 'dispossesed' soul, existing purposelessly in a purposeless world. Similarly there is also Salinger's eccentric Glass family, all of whom are wholly outsiders and provide a unique panorama of characters, brilliantly exposed and dissected by the author's pen. In *Franny and Zooey*, we meet with the sensitive and disgusted Franny, helplessly falling away from conventional life. Along with her is her caustic and audacious brother Zooey, ruthlessly tired of life's vanity and stupidities. In this book we are also introduced to Franny and Zooey's older brothers and would-be spiritual mentors, Buddy and Seymour, both of whose character portraits are expanded upon in Salinger's other works, *Raise High the Roofbeam Carpenters*, and *Seymour, an Introduction*; within these short stories we meet with these two towering intellectual and spiritual geniuses- the younger one, Buddy, who ends up living alone in a cabin in the woods, without a phone, and for the most part abandoning life, and his older brother, Seymour, who lives a brief life of seemingly divine insight and understanding, only to kill himself with a bullet through the head at age of thirty-one, despite the fact that, as his brother Buddy attests, he was a rare and exceptional *mukta*, or, god-knower.

I bring these characters- described artfully by Salinger's special slant on the craft of writing- up briefly, not because they will appear again in this work, but to offer to the reader a modern, literary analysis of individuals on the cusp of being spiritually 'finished', so to speak, only to find themselves more trapped in the world than if they had remained fully in the dark all along. I take Salinger's work on 'outsiders' to be a voice for the futility of life as we 'know' it. And so, keeping this in mind, the reader will understand better as we move along, why I am therefore setting out to propose that we are much better off by 'unknowing' it.

7 *The Outsider*, p25

147

mental defeat."[8]

Now, this 'harsh queerness' and 'harsh glare' will necessarily lead to the 'mental defeat' of a scientist, such as Wells (or anyone else so dependent on the reasoning mind), who finally must come begrudgingly to terms with his or her own incorrigible ignorance.

"All will be desperately lost in this sudden bedazzlement."
Rene Daumal

H.G. Wells aptly titled his last book- from which the quote noted above arises- *Mind at the End of Its Tether*. I say 'aptly' because for one who has struggled his whole life to understand and explain life, and then, at the eleventh-hour, to realize he understands nothing, it is logical that this non-understanding would appear as a bitter defeat, rather than as an ultimate success.

Any individual such as Wells, caught rapt in the grip of immanent exasperation, often becomes effectively incapacitated from this conceptual breakdown; and it is *existence* itself which is the debilitating enigma- because 'what is' is, and ...because one cannot understand it.

Sam Keen notes: "The primal source of wonder is not an object but the fact the mind is sometimes jarred into the realization that there is no necessary reason for the existence of the world or anything in it. ...In speaking of [this]...Tillich said that, viewed from the standpoint of the possibility of nonbeing, being is a mystery. However odd it may be linguistically or logically, there are states of mind in which the very existence of

---

8 *The Outsider*, p4

the world seems strange and miraculous..."[9]

It is as if a person is immobilized by awareness itself, by the transfixed vision of magnificence and confusion. And this is an event of either horror, or elation; when the mind is entirely freed the individual is either emancipated, or condemned by the terror of that freedom.

"This is in the end the only kind of courage that is required of us: the courage to face the strangest, most unusual, most inexplicable experiences that can meet us."
Rainer Maria Rilke[10]

It is a fine line, a razor's edge, between mysticism and madness. Yet whether the experience of suddenly awakening to the all-pervasive mystery of life- and to our own astoundingly comprehensive ignorance- leads the individual to the rapture of a god-intoxicated saint, to the tortured bottom of a whisky bottle, or to a life of lonely isolation- it is more or less the same experience, and is altered simply by the way in which it is dealt with: whether a person falls down in fright and nausea, or instead finds their 'sea legs' and learns to move with the rhythm of infinity.

It is my contention that this experience of incomprehension (which Wilson's outsiders found to be grounds for melancholy, madness, escapism, or suicide) is not an inherently tragic experience, but is, in fact, essential to the development of the higher self; we escape the confines of the limited life through the porthole of absurdity, and there we find not an event which misleads us out of life, but one that returns us

---

9 *Apology for Wonder*, p22
10 *Letters to a Young Poet*, p89

truly and finally to life, and therefore is not worthy of despair but ...of exaltation.

> *"The world is not only stranger than we suppose,*
> *it is stranger than we can suppose."*
> J.B.S. Haldane

In Dostoyevsky's book *The Idiot*, Prince Myshkin details the evolution of his undoing- from confusion, to suffering, to ecstasy: "...I'd experienced a series of bad and agonizing attacks...and...it grew worse...the fits came on several times in succession, I fell into a state of utter stupefaction, with complete loss of memory. Though my reason wasn't effected, the course of my logical thinking was interrupted, as it were, I couldn't connect more than two or three consecutive ideas. That's the impression I have retained. When the fits abated...I was in a state of unbearable melancholy, I remember; I was actually on the verge of tears all the time, in constant dismay and anxiety, and I was terribly effected by it all being so *alien* to me- that much I realized. The foreignness of it was crushing. [But] I emerged from my depression... I began to recover rapidly. Then each day grew more precious to me, and the passage of each new day made it all the more precious, so that I couldn't help noticing the fact. I would go to bed very pleased with the day, and awake the next morning feeling even happier. It would be very hard to say why that was so. ...At such moments I felt something calling me into the distance, and it would seem that if I were to walk straight ahead for a long, long time, and cross that distant line where the earth and sky met, I would find the key to everything and at once behold a new life a thousand times more thrilling and vibrant than ours."[11]

Myshkin is speaking, unknowingly perhaps, of a sublime process- the alchemical transmutation of the gross ore of consciousness into the pure gold. This shift, according to the terminology of alchemy, is the movement from the *nigredo* to *albedo* to *rubedo*.[12]

This immanent Art of alchemy is also adroitly written into the crucible of Rainer Maria Rilke's unique poetry and life. Excerpted sections from his *Duino Elegies*, which subtly document stages of the process, run along the same theme as the last quote:

---

11 *The Idiot*, p84-88

12 Of course, I do not suggest this as a summation of Alchemy, which is far more vast and complex than I could claim to propound upon here. However, there are aspects of the Art which absolutely require the loss of all that is known, and an entry into the dark unknown, in order to reach the light at the other side. A similar account to Myshkin's is given by Eckhart Tolle, in his brief autobiography at the beginning of his book *The Power of Now*. Excerpts run as follows: "Until my thirtieth year, I lived in a state of almost continuous anxiety interspersed with periods of suicidal depression. ...One night not long after my twenty-ninth birthday, I woke up in the early hours with a feeling of absolute dread. I had awoken up with such a feeling many times before, but this time it was more intense than it had ever been. ...everything felt so alien, so hostile, and so utterly meaningless that it created in me a deep loathing of the world. The most loathsome thing of all, however, was my own existence. ...I could feel that a deep longing for annihilation, for nonexistence, was now becoming much stronger than the instinctive desire to continue to live. ...I could feel myself being sucked into a void. It felt as if the void was inside myself rather than outside. Suddenly there was no more fear, and I let myself fall into the void. I have no recollection of what happened after that. ...I was awakened by the chirping of a bird outside the window. I had never heard such a sound before. My eyes were still closed, and I saw the image of a precious diamond. I opened my eyes. The first light of dawn was filtering through the curtains. Without any thought, I felt, I knew, that there is infinitely more to light than we realize. ...Tears came into my eyes. I got up and walked around the room. I recognized the room, and yet I knew that I had never truly seen it before. Everything was fresh and pristine, as if it had just come into existence. I picked up things, a pencil, an empty bottle, marveling at the beauty and aliveness of it all. That day I walked around the city in utter amazement at the miracle of life on earth, as if I had just been born into this world. ...[Later] a time came when, for a while, I was left with nothing on the physical plane. I had no relationships, no job, no home, no socially defined identity. I spent almost two years sitting on park benches in a state of the most intense joy." (p1-3)

151

"Of course, it is strange to inhabit the earth no longer,
to give up customs one barely had time to learn,
not to see roses and other promising Things
in terms of a human future; no longer to be
what one was in infinitely anxious hands; to leave
even one's own first name behind, forgetting it
as easily as a child abandons a broken toy.
Strange to no longer desire one's desires. Strange
To see meanings that clung together once floating away
In every direction. (*first elegy*)
...[But then] suddenly in this laborious nowhere, suddenly
the unsayable spot where the pure Too-little is transformed
incomprehensibly, leaps around and changes
into that empty Too-much;
where the difficult calculation
becomes numberless and resolved. (*fifth elegy*)
...Wasn't all this a miracle? Be astonished, Angel, for we
are this, O Great One; proclaim that we could achieve this,
my breath is too short for such praise. (*seventh elegy*)
...Look, I am living ...Superabundant being wells up in my
heart. (*ninth elegy*)"

The end of this lengthy verse by Rilke is certainly a description of the brighter side of the dark and unknown; he has come through unmiracle and reclaimed the miracle.

> *"A disorienting passage through 'the cloud of unknowing'*
> *may well be the initial test of our adequacy as individuals."*
> Stephen Larson[13]

---

13 *The Mythic Imagination*, p16

From this point on we see that the individual who has, through initiation into mystery, been turned into an 'outsider', may enter into a reversal and re-turn to become an 'insider', for now he or she is not painfully outside of the mystery of life, but is instead within it, and integral to it- a living part of the enigmatic whole.[14]

The 'immanence' of mystery, and the 'Great Art' of alchemy, as documented by Rilke and others, will be further discussed in the final chapter, when all the ingredients have been mixed into the cauldron, so to speak.

Leo Tolstoy's candid statements continue our theme: "Five years ago something very strange began to happen to me. At first I experienced moments of perplexity and arrest of life, as though I did not know how to live or what to do. ...Then these moments of perplexity recurred oftener and oftener. ...I felt that what I had been standing on had broken down, and that I had nothing left under my feet. What I had lived on no longer existed, and I had nothing left to live on."[15]

Yet Tolstoy would go on to become one of the greatest novelists of history, and would also write a book on his political and psychological thought called, interestingly enough, *The Kingdom of God is Within You*, which would be read by the likes of Mahatma Gandhi, and would end up influencing the whole subcontinent of India's non-violent revolution and emancipation.

Therefore, the experience of having 'nothing under our feet'- of all that we thought we knew suddenly revealing itself as unknowable- can lead towards two possible outcomes: crisis, or completion.

14This accomplishment by the adept is described by Henry Miller as such: "He divines that the great secret will never be apprehended but incorporated into his very substance. He has to make himself a part of the mystery, live *in* it as well as with it." (*Sexus*)
15 *Life of Tolstoy*, by Aylmer Maude, p384-385

"Having to believe that the world is mysterious and unfathomable was the expression of a warrior's innermost predilection. Without it, he had nothing."
Don Juan[16]

As with all great hero and heroine journeys, there must be inner trial if there is to be inner reward.

Chuck Spezzano, in his commentary on *The Enlightenment Cards*, describes this stage of the epic as such: "The meaninglessness and the anguish this engenders- because everything has turned grey and to ashes- can be a great opportunity for you. While many people die in the realms of meaninglessness, it could be one of the places where you make some of your greatest strides in consciousness. ...[For] when meaninglessness is seen from a high spiritual perspective, it is the realization that the world actually does not have any meaning. [Yet] the ego attempts to lure us off and show us that the world *does* have meaning: 'Come right this way! Step right up! The greatest show on earth is about to begin! Come to the sideshow! You will find something interesting that will keep you entertained here!' Of course, because this is not true, you are eventually brought back to the experience of meaninglessness once again, but this time it is through disappointment in the world. However, meaninglessness is actually a place which is very close to realization, awakening and enlightenment."[17]

For those people who are tightly wrapped in a comfortable life, with many desires or responsibilities, such an

---

16 *Tales of Power*, by Carlos Castaneda, p115
17 *The Enlightenment Book*, p46. Ramtha corroborates this thought, claiming: "...I wouldn't doubt that one day you will sit back aghast and wonder, *Am I losing it?* ...No, you're gaining it. What you are losing...is the fogbank of illusion- you're gaining the clarity of reality. The reality is the unknown." (*Destination Freedom II*, p161)

154

experience of meaninglessness can lead to their downfall- for it destroys their false life completely; they are the ones who, finding themselves fallen into quicksand, thrash wildly about in an attempt to extricate themselves, only to sink deeper and deeper into the mire.

Yet for those who are inherently more elastic, more capable of 'turning on a dime', so to speak, of recognizing the virtue of a 'real' experience, and thus who are also capable of 'letting go', of enjoying the wild ride of inexplicable awe, and then of finding the wherewithal to go forth in life with this new experience as their living corner-stone while rejecting all past structures, these are the ones who will not only survive intact, but will fly instead of drowning, and will flourish from the very same event which caused others to crumble.

Aleister Crowley notes: "...the best of men, the free men, do not consider the matter in such terms at all. Whatever horrors may afflict the soul, whatever abominations may excite the loathing of the heart, whatever terrors may assail the mind, the answer is the same at every stage: 'How splendid is the Adventure!'"[18]

There it is. Life is a bewildering event, of that there is no argument. It is simply then a matter of whether we choose to see life as a miraculous adventure, or a tragic misadventure.

"I had to grow foul with knowledge, realize the futility of everything, smash everything, grow desperate, then humble, then sponge myself off the slate, as it were, in order to recover my authenticity. I had to arrive at the brink and then take a leap in the dark."
Henry Miller[19]

---

18 *The Book of Thoth*, p113
19 *The Wisdom of the Heart.* Commisseratingly, David Icke wrote: "When you start on

Jose Ortega Y Gasset explains this outlook, albeit from a different angle; he writes: "The man with the clear head is the man who frees himself from those 'fantastic' ideas and looks life in the face, realizes that everything is problematic, and feels himself lost. And this is the simple truth- that to live is to feel oneself lost... He who does not really feel himself lost, is without remission; that is to say, he never finds himself, never comes up against his own reality."[20]

Reality is a crazy mystery, and we ourselves are the crazy mystery, but instead of seeking erroneously for reason and sanity to it all, we simply need to shift about, grant ourselves the license to be absurd, implausible, indefinable, and rare. It is then that we can look upon ourselves as the inexplicable, privileged miracles that we truly are. It is then that the adventure begins.

This acceptance of such inextricable 'lostness' would lead Carlos Castaneda to confess: "I was not afraid but baffled. ...The loopholes in my reason were so gigantic that either I had to repair them or I had to dispose of my reason altogether. ...What I experienced at the moment of that realization was such an intense astonishment that all I could do was stare, stupefied."[21]

"Good, good" retorted don Juan to Castaneda, "I've told you that the true art of a warrior is to balance terror and wonder."[22]

---

the spiritual journey, when you open your mind and your heart to other possibilities, all hell often breaks loose in your life. Your life starts to fall apart. There is a good reason for this." (*Lifting the Veil*, p92)

20 *The Revolt of the Masses*, p157

21 *Tales of Power*, p51,148

22 *ibid*, p91. And the anonymous voice from Elsa Barker's *Letters from a Living Dead Man* implores: "Oh, do not be afraid of giving rein to your imagination! It is the wonderful things which are really true; the commonplace things are nearly all false. When a great thought lifts you by the hair, do not cling hold of the solid earth. Let go.

There is a point in life when all theories, ideas, proofs, and arguments fall irrevocably impotent, and the individual, determinedly bent hard upon comprehending his or her life in the implausible cosmos, will suddenly sense that none of what has been told to them about life is true; that Life, in fact, is not about understanding, but about living, and that the more we try to understand ...the less we live. For there is no wisdom in trying to understand what is not understandable. And there is less wisdom in imagining that one understands what one does not understand. And there is less wisdom still in retreating from the realization that we absolutely 'do not know', and shrinking back into a secure, limited lie, instead of accepting the confounding Enigma, and thus embracing life's majesty completely, because of the very fact that it is well beyond our limited comprehension. This is Life. Ours is the choice whether to obscure it with words, or worship it with wonder.

"O gnashing teeth of earth, where would it all lead but some sweet golden eternity, to prove that we've all been wrong, to prove that proving was nil... I realized, 'there is no answer'. I didn't know anything any more, I didn't care, and it didn't matter, and suddenly I felt really free."
Jack Kerouac[23]

As the phoenix rises from its own ashes, and the snake sheds its worn out old skin, so must we molt mentally if we are to live, and die, and live again.

Excerpts from Sam Keen's *Apology for Wonder* eloquently document this process of death and resurrection:

...If one goes fast and high enough, one may behold the inconceivable." (p211)
23 *Dharma Bums*, p240

"When something explodes into awareness and shatters our ordinary categories of understanding, it quite naturally creates mental and emotional dis-ease and puzzlement. What is this novel star that has suddenly appeared on my horizon? Who is this stranger who speaks so unexpectedly out of the mouth of my wife? Why is it that the rose I observed yesterday and the day before today confronts me with a miracle of redness? ...When we are wonderstruck our certainties dissolve, and we are precipitated suddenly into contingency. We are alike a man waking in the middle of the night in a strange hotel room and not being able, for the moment, to remember where he is. ...Wonder...insofar as it disrupts our proven ways of coping with the world...is menacing; insofar as it offers the promise of renewing novelty, it is desirable and fascinating. If we attend to the strict meanings of the words, we may describe the heart of the experience of wonder as an *awful-promising surprise*. ...The imagery of apocalypse and resurrection is integral to the experience of wonder. Every wonder-event involves a cognitive crucifixion; it disrupts the system of meanings that secures the identity of the ego. To wonder is to die to the self, to cease imposing categories, and to surrender the self... Refreshment or resurrection leaves us reborn but unable to articulate an adequate testimony. There is nothing new to say about the world...only a new ability to celebrate it..."[24]

This 'disorientation and reorientation' is the psychological equivalent of the alchemical formula *solve et coagula* (dis-solve and re-combine); everything is taken apart and re-made. This, as has been said, can be destabilizing, to say the least. And yet it is essential, and unavoidable, and requires only our acceptance of the process in order to see it through to completion. In a state of wonder, no piece of the paradigm can

---

24 *Apology for Wonder* p28-31. Osho suggests that this is the ultimate meaning of the resurrection- "...a death of the old and a birth of the new." (*The Rebel*, p33)

endure.

Once we have made it through the 'dark night of the soul', then we are healed from the tortures of the mind's misconceptions. This is when we are "...opened to the ecstasy of Creation", as Ida Mingle described it.[25]

It is here that we find some respite, for we no longer care what society cares for, and no longer understand what others understand. Here we are finished with the confines of the limited mind. Here is where, if we a strong enough to be nothing, ...here is where we are free.[26]

"From that day onward every moment brought me its freshness as an ineffable gift, so that I lived in an almost perpetual state of passionate wonder. I became intoxicated with extreme rapidity, and went about in a sort of daze."
Andre Gide[27]

Judith Handelsman wrote of her rapturous experience,

---

25 *Steps in the Way*, p89
26 D.T. Suzuki wrote: "...When this breaking out is too precipitous and violent, the mind may lose its balance more or less permanently... In most cases the effect is not very grave and the crisis may pass without leaving deep marks. But in some characters, either through their inherent tendencies or on account of the influence of environment upon their plastic constitution, the spiritual awakening stirs them up to the very depths of their personality. This is the time you will be asked to choose between the 'Everlasting No' and the 'Everlasting Yea. ...Being so long accustomed to the oppression [of the intellect], the mental inertia becomes hard to remove. In fact it has gone down deep into the roots of our own being, and the whole structure of personality is to be overturned. The process of reconstruction is stained with tears and blood. ...But it is only after such pain and turbulence that all the internal impurities are purged and one is born with quite a new outlook on life." (*Essays in Zen Buddhism*, p29-31)
27 Paraphrasing Socrates, Osho relates: "This morning- this very morning- something tremendous has happened to me: all knowledge has appeared as futile. I am awakened. The sleep of knowledge is no longer there; I am no longer dreaming. And now I know only one thing for certain: that I don't know anything." (*Ecstasy*, p33)

159

exclaiming: "'Victory for the forces of good! Here, here!' I cried, jumping up and down, dancing in place, cheering...for the wonders of the invisible world I had just entered. ...I allowed magic into my life and had opened the way for more to come."[28]

Thus the lucky, brave, or innocent individual who receives this intoxication of absolute wonder- of the complete non-understanding of all that 'is', including their own self- no longer needs a reasonable explanation of life, because they are wholly free from the mind's interventions; for them there is nothing gained by trying to apprehend an explanation ...of the unexplainable. Ideas no longer matter, knowledge is gone for good, and the whole of life swells and returns to its original, pristine spectacularness.

"...I start to float away,
and the whole world seems very strange,
in a pleasant kind of way."
Blue Rodeo[29]

Though our journey into the realm of mystery may begin as a frightening cataclysm, eventually the loss of understanding- if we are accepting enough of the process- may take over and we may begin to find our 'footing', our balance, so to speak, and what originally seemed a chaotic, turbulent, nauseating, ride, becomes a fluid, invigorating, familiar euphoria.

It is now a joy to positively accept our non-understanding, to embrace it, and in doing so we begin to acknowledge its validity more readily even than our day-to-day realities. We begin to believe that the world of men has been

---

28 *Growing Myself*, p23-25
29 from their album *Five Days in July*

horribly untruthful to us, and that we have finally returned to our senses. We ease back into ourselves. Everything becomes new and spectacular. Nothing exists that is not implausible. A benign, peaceful reverie may begin to grow within our lives.

This is the gentler side of rapture, easing into the comforting unknowableness of all and everything, and willfully succumbing to the blessed sublime intoxication of the thoughtless presence of being.[30]

"The Seer is lost in wonder, which is Peace"
Aleister Crowley[31]

And the Indian mystic, Sri Ramakrishna, so often found alone, caught rapt in rapture- or *samadhi*, as it is referred to in the East- described the experience as such: "In ecstasy a man remains dumb with wonder…[he] forgets the external world with all its charms and attractions; even one's own body which is so dear to one, is easily forgotten."[32]

Rapture, therefore, is not necessarily an event of surging, emotional exuberance, but is often the more placid experience of being 'rapt' in wonder; it is then more similar to the stillness of awe, than the volatility of ecstasy. And though rapture may begin as a 'mind-blowing' sensation, it may also evolve into a passively enjoyable continuum.

---

30 Sam Keen suggests that: "A mature sense of wonder does not need the constant titillation of the sensation to keep it alive. It is most often called forth by a confrontation with the mysterious depth of meaning at the heart of the familiar and quotidian." (*Apology for Wonder*, p23)
31 *Thoth*, p143. And so, "When all the words and meanings stop, it is purity, peace", stated Swamiji Shyam (Talks, Mar 1999)
32 *Memoirs of Ramakrishna*, p59

"The wonderment of pristine cognitions is the path of no-more-learning when one has come to the end of one's labors..."
Longchenpa[33]

As such, Richard Bach exultantly admitted: "For a moment I tasted my new ignorance, shifted it on my tongue. What am I to do? Whatever will become of me? ...a surprise new pleasure broke and surged over me like a cool breaker from far deeps. I didn't know what I'd do!"[34]

That is, if we are ready to let all thought and knowledge slip carelessly away from our minds and lives we shall neither find ourselves sitting in a corner of a room, cringing against the staggering reality before us, nor, through weakness or discomfort will we ever again need to return to the horrid mind-frame of words, conceptions, presumptions and all that separates us from our true selves. We shall instead bask comfortably in the dynamic, wordless, eternal warm glow of the voiceless song of our beings.

Russell Hoban's unique character, Riddley Walker, comes forth with his own bewildered and yet accepting appreciation of this new essence; in the full, apocalyptic colloquialisms of his voice, he gargles out, "My head begun to feal like it wer widening like circles on water I dint know if it wud ever stop I dint know where the end of it wud be. The stranger it took me the mor I felt at hoam with it. The mor I fealt Iwd be long where ever it wer widening me to."[35]

And Clarice Lispector describes this acquiescence about one of her characters, writing: "[He] no longer asked for the

33 *Kindly Bent to Ease Us*
34 *The Bridge Across Forever*, p15
35 *Riddley Walker*, p 116

name of things. It was enough for him to recognize them in the dark- And rejoice, clumsily."[36]

So when we are strong in the foothold of ignorance, all of existence will blend into the fabulous harmony of its infinite, singular mystery; we shall worship life in the act of living it, and with that we shall return to wholeness in the union of our awe.

"...it came to me that to love the mystery surrounding us is the final and only sanction of human existence."
Hugh MacLennan[37]

It is a pathless way back to rapture, and it is available to all of us; and so it is now merely a choice for each of us to rise up and follow, to walk or to wallow; it is up to each of us to find the beauty and miracle again in life, and in ourselves, and to deliver our gospel, however impossibly we may, to our unrapturous fellows still trapped in an unwonderful day.

As Arthur Machen contends: "Some have declared that it lies within our choice to gaze continually upon a world of equal or even greater wonder and beauty. It is said by these that the experiments of the alchemists in the Dark Ages...are, in fact, related not to the transmutation of metals, but to the transmutation of the entire Universe. ...This method, or art, or science, or whatever we choose to call it...is simply concerned to restore the delights of the primal Paradise; to enable men, if they will, to inhabit a world of joy and splendor. It is perhaps possible that there is such an experiment, and that there are some

---

36 *The Apple in the Dark*, p319
37 Likewise, Rainer Maria Rilke exalted: "Unknowing before the heavens of my life, I stand in wonder."

who have made it."[38]

And so, finding his own philosopher's stone, Jack Kerouac announced: "...I would be strange and ragged and like the Prophet who has walked across the land to bring the dark Word, and the only Word I had was "Wow!"[39]

*****

38 quoted in *Tales of Horror and the Supernatural*, p302
39 *On the Road*

CHAPTER 10: The Mad and the Mystic

"I love everything that flows, everything that has time in it and becoming, that brings us back to the beginning where there is never end...all that is fluid, melting, dissolute and dissolvent, all the pus and dirt that in flowing is purified, that loses its sense of origin, that makes the great circuit towards death and dissolution. The great incestuous wish is to flow on, one with time, to merge the great image of the beyond with the here and now. A fatuous, suicidal wish that is constipated by words and paralyzed by thought."

Henry Miller[1]

"I am not referring to the simple-minded. The desirable thing is to be intelligent and not to understand. It is a strange blessing, like experiencing madness without being insane. It is quiet indifference, and idiotic gentleness."

Clarice Lispector[2]

"I should have liked to sow Doubt into the entrails of the Globe, to imbue its substance with Doubt, to enthrone Doubt where the mind never penetrated, and before reaching the marrow of mankind, to shake the calm of stones, to introduce there the insecurity and the anguish of the heart. ...As men cherish a secret craving to repudiate themselves, I should have provoked self-betrayal everywhere, plunged innocence into stupor, multiplied disloyalties, kept the multitude from wallowing in the compost heap of certitudes."

E.M Cioran[3]

"The mind that is capable of saying "I do not know", is in the only state in which anything can be discovered."

Jiddu Krishnamurti[4]

---

1 *Tropic of Cancer*, p258
2 *JdoB*, Feb1/69
3 *A Short History of Decay*, p159
4 Talks in Ojai, Aug 1955

As can be seen from the last chapter, the profound experience of mystery is often accompanied by a feeling of instability that, in its most unchecked aspect, ends up in madness. And yet, as Pascal pointed out: "Men are so necessarily mad, that to not be mad would result in another form of madness."

And so, before we proceed with the culminating chapters of the book, let us, for the sheer crazy pleasure of it, take a brief stomp through the divine madhouse; let us hear from some of the individuals who may not have come through the death and resurrection with all their parts intact, but who came through nonetheless.

It is well known that there is a fine line between genius and insanity, but perhaps there is even a finer line between genius and ignorance, lucid ignorance; the person who coherently loses all concept of life, who intentionally, or not, forgets what it means to 'be', ends up dwelling, as we have seen, in the precarious realm between ecstasy and derangement.

"Ever wonder if there's a difference between having a mystical experience and completely losing your mind?"
Michael Peddie[5]

Well, perhaps there is not much of a difference after all.

In the previous chapter I briefly mentioned the darker aspects of a person's tragic encounter with the upheaval of wonderment- where the 'outsider' was seen as an individual who had not properly assimilated novel realizations into their existence. On the other side of the coin, however, there exist the 'crazies' who have lived abundantly (well, some who did, some

---

5 *Where Whales Love to Boogie*, p1

166

who didn't) and joyously in their new perspective, despite being permanently stationed on the fringe of life. These heroes of sane ignorance are the wise madmen and madwomen in this chapter, who, from time to time, maintain enough functional control of their faculties to record for the rest of us the annihilation of every solidity, every certainty, and every truth, for they have come to exist defiantly in the limbo of freedom, madness, and wonder.

One of these individuals, Fyodor Dostoyevsky, has done a remarkable job of describing the internal struggles of those who have seen the precariousness of our reality. From his aptly titled novel, *The Idiot*, to his not-so-short story *Notes From Underground*, to his brilliantly succinct and inspiring *The Dream of a Ridiculous Man*, he provides us with a collage of disparate, idiosyncratic 'fools', as it were. We shall not here delve into these works, but instead be satisfied with Henry Miller's description of Dostoyevsky himself, which is as lucid as Dostoyevsky's characters were strange. Of this rare 'outsider', Miller wrote: "Dostoyevsky was the sum of all those contradictions which either paralyze a man or lead him to the heights. There was no world too low for him to enter, no place too high for him to ascend. He went the whole gamut, from the abyss to the stars. ...It is a pity that we shall never have the opportunity to read again or see a man placed at the very core of mystery, and by his flashes not merely illuminating things for us, but showing us the depth, the immensity of the darkness."[6]

At 'the core of mystery', when all the walls, repressions, denials, and lies crumble to useless pieces around the lucky or forsaken individual (as they did for Dostoyevsky, who survived numerous crises, including almost being executed, and many torturous years in the hopeless gulag), there is no hidden meaning which bubbles to the fore, only an obvious non-meaning ensconcing all and everything; an essential,

---

6 *Tropic of Cancer*, p230

immense non-meaning, for non-meaning is the essence of the core.

"I am at home in the marvelous. Absolutely at home.
The unknown, the mysterious, the exotic,
the strange, the never-lived-before, the difficult."
Anais Nin[7]

At the throbbing core of life, mystery suddenly becomes unavoidably obvious ...because meaning is now absolutely obscured. It is this descent from the surface of reasonableness, to the unreasonable center, which is the hero or heroine's true journey. Heroic clarity then comes from simply accepting the furthest extent of one's irrevocable confusion one can endure.

Along with Dostoyevsky noted above, Henry Miller wrote about many of his other heroes as well, most of whom were mad artists, and his words convey the essential predicament of this chapter; he relates: "I see this other race of individuals ransacking the universe, turning everything upside down, their feet always moving in blood and tears, their hands always empty, always clutching and grasping for the beyond, for the god out of reach: slaying everything within reach in order to quiet the monster that gnaws at their vitals. I see that when they tear their hair with the effort to comprehend, to seize this forever unattainable, I see that when they bellow like crazed beasts and rip and gore, I see that this is right, that there is no other path to pursue. ...anything less shuddering...less mad, less intoxicated...is counterfeit. ...Let us have...a world of natural fury, of passion, action, drama, dreams, madness, a world that

---

7 *Diaries* 1934-1939

produces ecstasy and not dry farts."[8]

Ah, but what of propriety, respectability, and convention? Indeed, what of these? In the pursuit of ecstasy and wonder, there is no room for petty concerns or approbation. And that applies as much inwardly, as it does out. Hence Ernest Becker described Rudolph Otto's tangle with his own shattered psyche, stating: "[He] talked about the terror of the world, the feeling of overwhelming awe, wonder, and fear in the face of creation- the miracle of it, the *mysterium tremendum et fascinosum* of each thing, of the fact that there are things at all."[9]

When the mind comes undone, the ego comes undone with it, as we recall from the necessary relationship between epistemological and psychological surrender.

The fact is that those who come to this critical loss of all cohesion find that there is much that is perceived by non-understanding alone; sublime phenomena requiring perversions of themselves in order to be vouchsafed to us. Which is to say, as it is by vegetation that we eat soil, air, sunlight, and dung, so it is through not-knowing that we apprehend the unknown. And therefore, if we seek to have a relationship with what cannot be known, then it is obvious that we cannot expect to exist in the security of 'knowing'.

> *"...to have that secret that I still couldn't understand, I would again give my life. I had risked the world in search of the question that comes after the answer. ...I hadn't found a human answer to the enigma. But much more, oh much more: I had found the enigma itself."*
> Clarice Lispector[10]

---

8 *Tropic of Cancer*, p231
9 *The Denial of Death*, p49
10 *The PASSION according to G.H.*, p130

Without this catastrophic intelligent ignorance, we might know a great deal of little knowings, and yet know nothing of the immense unknown.

To come to such a perspective (or non-perspective) is one of the ultimate human sacrifices (recall here the *Bhagavad Gita's* claim that "Better than the sacrifice of any objects is the sacrifice of wisdom.") Thus, Benjamin Tucker describes this willful sacrifice, concluding: "It is in the rehabilitation of position that the succumbing power refuses to be defined, and in the process (if the process is fabulous enough) emerges from its own emerging, writhes in the passage that is omnidirectional, pursues the intensity so furiously that the conundrum becomes the home." (brackets are author's)[11]

Therefore, to attempt any understanding at this rarified level of non-understanding ...is to misunderstand. Genius does not discern truth for us, it exposes us to mystery.

Only mystery is true to form; only an enigma is seen as what it truly 'is'- whatever that may be. There is no such thing as understanding, only more sublime levels of non-understanding, or more tragic levels of misunderstanding; the greater the apparent understanding, the greater the misunderstanding.

> *"Back in those days, everything was simpler*
> *and more confused."*
> Jim Morrison

To arrive at the precious and perilous realm of incohesion, of unawareness, we must be willing and brave; we

---

11 *Of*

must allow the veneer of being to immolate completely; nothing of what we hold onto or believe in can survive a single moment of true, apocalyptic wonder. All the monuments fall in the earthquake of incognition; it may mean that our old well-ordered lives are ruined completely, that we are done for, if we come to rupturous, rapturous non-understanding correctly. Nothing remains of life as it was imagined to be- for finally we have matured beyond the pablum of knowledge. That is the way of the mad and the mystic.

Lispector describes this maturity in one of her characters, writing: "With this enormous courage the man had finally stopped being intelligent."[12] Which is to say, to give yourself away to the mystery that you are, to float upward like a balloon without a mooring, to unrecognize existence with a fearless glance unshaken by the nebulous infinity, is to die and be born again, at every moment, without a clue what is happening to you.

"It is the logic of Illogic. And this is all one can say.
...My lucid unreason is not afraid of chaos."
Antonin Artaud[13]

Though Artaud is one of the mystical madmen who perhaps lost it too completely in the end (spending nine years in an asylum in France, where he aggressively declared, "I am a fanatic, I am not a madman"), at least he went down swinging.

Anais Nin wrote, after meeting Artaud, "All I could see that evening was his revolt against interpretations. He was

---

12 *The Apple in the Dark*
13 *The Artaud Reader*

impatient with their presence, as if they prevented him from exaltation."[14] And so he was a hero indeed, forfeiting all reasonableness and caution for one thing and one thing only-ecstasy.

Wonder for some individuals, then, is not merely an experience to be had and then quickly 'gotten over', as it were; it is instead an outlook which must be sedulously integrated until it becomes a fanatical disposition demanding intimacy with the unfathomableness of being, and this is the power which redeems all of creation from the bounds of logic and reason.

"The non-mysterious concerns of human beings may be drawn as clearly as the outlines of this page. ...What is to be inscribed here but the disgust of generations linked like propositions in the sterile fatality of a syllogism?"
E.M. Cioran [15]

We see that when the will to honesty overpowers the need for the security of understanding, only then will the exasperated individual stand his or her ground; only then will a person hold firm in the acceptance that the history of knowledge and learning is but a cowardly attempt to orient oneself within an unimaginable event- life! To finally come to terms with such a realization is to isolate oneself from the claustrophobia of man's 'reason', and to believe in one's vision, despite what all others claim you should see.

This 'new' madness is the sanity of wonder. And only those strong enough to withstand the tide of mankind's misconceptions, and to walk clean through without succumbing

---

14 *Anais Nin's Diaries,* 1934-1938
15 *A Short History of Decay,* p72

172

to the taint, only they shall be counted as the Keepers of the Mystery.

Osho provides us with a definition of this type, stating: "Strangeness of a thing immediately shakes you out of the rut of unconsciousness. ...if someone can go mad consciously, it would be a great experience; no other experience could be greater than this. ...it is in such a situation that a feeling of utter strangeness overwhelms you... You suddenly find that all connections, all communications...have snapped, that all bridges have broken, and all adjustments have collapsed. You find that everything relevant has become irrelevant; the day to day relevance of things is lost altogether."[16]

Again, wonder is not about seeing spectacles that are wonderful, but wonder is instead a living function of the individual's openness, which is independent of any specific phenomena- because it includes everything; magic is a perspective, not an occurrence. Wonder is woven into the immanent fabric of the wondering mind, not in the outward recognition of something wonderful; it is the individual's inward ability to un-recognize everything at once, in a euphoric implosion of non-interpretation.

From another individual who went the full distance into Mystery, so to speak, we have, from Vaslav Nijinski's diary, "I want the death of mind. ...The mind is stupidity, but wisdom is God."[17]

We shall meet with Nijinski again in the final chapter. It is said that in the final stages of his insanity (or perhaps sanity, as it were) he was found giving his money away on the street, and claiming that he had suffered more than Christ. Whatever the reality of his experience, there is no doubt from his diary that he, like Artaud, went so far away from the profane understanding

---

16 *Kundalini*, p201
17 *Nijinski's Diaries*, p47

of mankind, that he could not get back; neither of them could any longer participate conventionally in a world which was far below their understandings (or non-understanding) of life. Their manias were the passions of men awoken in a prison who believed that they alone knew all others were in prison as well. And that prison is the mind.

> *"...everything is distorted and displaced*
> *as soon as it understands itself."*
> Heinrich von Kleist[18]

Is it not our habit to distort everything, especially ourselves, by assuming to understand them? It is our pathos, our temerity, or caution, or demise.

And therefore, recognizing this, when finally we do confront ourselves with complete openness and candor, we must struggle not to turn quickly away, having found that we do not actually know who or what we are. Instead we must remain there, right in the eye of the hurricane, fully intimate with the self's bewilderment and confusion. We must "keep that don't know mind" when it matters most- when it is our own 'I' of which we know nothing.

Cioran stated: "When we perceive ourselves existing we have the sensation of a stupefied madman who surprises his own lunacy and vainly seeks to give it a name."[19]

What is required of mystical madmen, or madwomen, is to forge relentlessly into the unknown, no longer into the known; to accept over and over again that indeed we are all lost- that we

---

18 Kleist ended his tenure in wonderful madness with suicide, so we can perhaps count him as one who went too far.
19 *A Short History of Decay*, p104

understand nothing of the world or ourselves, and then to have the endurance to expect no reward, no solution, no final understanding, but only the need for more exasperation, more uncertainty, more incapacity.

"If the fool would continue his folly, he would become wise", wrote William Blake in his *Proverbs of Hell*. And the lucky corollary to Blake's aphorism is: if the wise man would continue his wisdom, he would become a fool.

If we are passionate and mad enough, the more we seek to understand the more we realize we do not understand, and eventually we cease to seek, and instead we just 'are'- we just live in the uncertain, absurd, implausible, inconceivable void. Indeed, the wise person who continues on with wisdom must necessarily fall ...dumb.

Hence Cioran finally admitted: "And for having sought to be a sage such as never was, I am only a madman among the mad..."[20]

So be it. It is the natural outcome of the ardent seeker- to come to awe through a short-circuited intelligence; for to stare into oneself with brutal honesty is to destroy all images and conclusions about what one is, or what one is supposed to be. That is all that is required- the honesty to unflinchingly be one's true, inconceivable self, despite the perilous, ignominious outcome. One who needs to see external miracles in order to believe in the miraculous, is a hopeless candidate for catastrophic, redemptive awe.

"Blessed are the cracked, for they shall let in the light."
Unknown[21]

20 *A Short History of Decay*, p180
21 *Utne Reader*, Aug 1998

Blessed indeed. Beatitudes abound in the sinless humility of irrevocable confusion.

"For there is no progression in the notion of universal vanity, nor conclusion", argued the loquacious Cioran, "and as far as we venture in such ruminations, our knowledge makes us no gain: it is in its present state as rich and as void as its point of departure. It is a surcease within the incurable, a leprosy of the mind, a revelation by stupor."[22]

Knowledge is vanity; to imagine that we 'know' is to beseech the universe to endure the absence of our inherent essence- the ecstasy of fools.

Fools we are, fools we were, and fools we shall be, yet only a very few of us are brave, or wild, or uninhibited, or oblivious enough to play the role of the jester in the Palace of Wonders we live within. Henry Miller describes one who took this role- of divine lunacy- as a vocation: "At the foot of the ladder reaching to the moon, Auguste would sit in contemplation, his smile fixed, his thoughts far away. This simulation of ecstasy, which he had brought to perfection, always impressed the audience as the summation of the incongruous. The great favorite had many tricks up his sleeve but this one was inimitable. Never before had a buffoon thought to depict the miracle of ascension."[23]

To be a fool because you are a fool is one thing, to willingly express your foolishness so as to enlighten others to their own ridiculousness is a whole new realm of sainthood.

Thomas Merton records this 'sacrifice' by one of the Desert Fathers, who had written: "One of the elders said: Either fly as far as you can from men, or else, laughing at the world and

---

22 *A Short History of Decay*, p88
23 *the smile at the foot of the ladder*

the men who are in it, make yourself a fool in many things."[24]

So it is with the likes of Charlie Chaplin, Groucho Marx, Woody Allen, Mr. Bean, Monty Python's Flying Circus, and so on; the jocular exposure of our limitless stupidity is the mark of artistic rarity. These actors not only make us laugh, they show us who we truly are, for "Anyone who thinks he is not a fool shows his ignorance."[25]

"Some people never go crazy/
what truly horrible lives they must lead."
Charles Bukowski

To not grasp for respectable perspectives, nor reputable lives, but to hold fast in the trenches of ignorance, this is the heroism of the day. So it is that courage and endurance are needed by anyone perspicacious enough to see their journey through to the disastrous realm of unmeaning.[26]

We must all endure this route, in one way or another, to one extremity or another, for the true self is eventually born only from a sarcophagus containing the remains of all the corpses we once were, and which we, ourselves, did kill, with wise ignorance. The murderer is the murdered. Man is his own sacrifice, and his own mercy; man is his own meat. The mind is an abattoir, wonder is a knife.

Cioran declares this process for us, writing: "The artist abandoning his poem, exasperated by the indigence of words, prefigures the confusion of the mind discontented with the

---

24 *The Wisdom of the Desert*
25 Hasidic lore
26 "The knack for being acutely conscious of the puzzle of his own and any *thing's* existence is a troubled blessing [for Butler]", described Thomas Jeffers of Samuel Butler. (*Samuel Butler Revalued*, p117)

context of the existent. Incapacity to organize the elements- as stripped of meaning and savor as the words which express them- leads to the revelation of the void."[27]

To paraphrase this, if I may: our false meanings, false lives, and false selves cannot survive under the pressure of our own relentless scrutiny; we disappear into mystery under our own fiery gaze.

Which is to say, there is, for the mad and the mystic, no such thing as intelligence, only cold-blooded honesty.

"I want, once and for all, *not* to know many things", bellowed the wearisome Nietzsche, sundered apart between the warring armies of megalomania, syphilis, and genius.

We must, if we are to find what these individuals have found (though perhaps not to suffer what they have suffered), heroically return our limited interpretations back to the glorious enigma of being; just as a growing child would hand their training-wheels back to their parents; though we must do this not because we are necessarily ready to ride, but because ...we are ready to crash.

"The purpose of life is to bring us closer to those secrets, and madness is the only means."
Kahlil Gibran[28]

We must fearlessly surrender to the collapse of all our conceptual armaments, perhaps even allowing ourselves to dissipate into the helpless shamelessness of drooling morons, and gaping fools.

"Such is the effect of coming face to face with the living

---

27 *A Short History of Decay*, p79
28 *Letters*, p62

mystery of God", admitted Kallistos Ware, "we are assailed by dizziness; all the familiar footholds vanish, and there seems nothing for us to grasp."

And from H. Rider Haggard: "For the mind wearies easily when it strives to grapple with the Infinite, and to trace the footsteps of the Almighty as he strides from sphere to sphere, or deduce His purpose from His works. Such things are not for us to know... Too much wisdom would perchance blind our imperfect sight, and too much strength would make us drunk, and overweight our feeble reason till it fell [hence the 'Fall'], and we were drowned in the depths of our own vanity. For what is the first result of man's increased knowledge interpreted from Nature's book by the persistent nature of his purblind effort? Is it not but too often to make him question the existence of his Maker, or indeed of any intelligent purpose beyond his own? The truth is veiled, because we could no more look upon her glory than we can upon the sun. It would destroy us. Full knowledge is not for man as man is here, for his capacities, which he is apt to think so great, are indeed but small. The vessel is soon filled, and, were one-thousandth part of the unutterable and silent wisdom that directs the rolling of those shining spheres, and the force which makes them roll, pressed into it, it would be shattered into fragments."[29]

Indeed, our reason must be shattered into fragments if we are to witness the unreasonable.

And now, if you do not accept these accounts of the blessedness of mad wisdom, perhaps we should go directly to the Source for corroboration: "In order to truly know God, you have to be out of your mind", says God.[30]

Which is to say, you have to 'lose your mind' if you would have 'no mind' and thus be able to know the unknowable.

---

29 *SHE*, p118
30 *Conversations with God*, by Neale Donald Walsch, p94

*"I ended by finding something sacred
in the disorder of my mind."*
Rimbaud

Recalling that the English word 'mystery' is a direct translation from the original Greek word for 'sacred', we can see that to not allow mystery into our lives is to desecrate (de-secret) all of life. To exist without awe is a sacrilege.

For "The hallmark, then, of the advanced religious, nonsectarian or any other", states J.D. Salinger, "...the hallmark most commonly identifying this person is that he very frequently behaves like a fool, even an imbecile."[31]

Perhaps this is the reason why Jiddu Krishnamurti was constantly stating that one must give up the desire for respectability if one is to progress towards reality; that is, one must not worry about being respectable, because only madness will set one free.

As such, David Goddard claims: "The enlightened sage is one who has attained cosmic consciousness- who is a fool as the world judges things and is free from the illusion of separateness, liberated from all appearances and limitations."[32]

And Osho describes a god-enlightened being as such: "...he was a madman- all religious people are mad. Mad, because they don't trust reason. Mad, because they love life. Mad, because they can dance and they can sing. Mad, because to them life is not a question, not a problem to be solved but a mystery into which one has dissolved. ...I am waiting for the day you are

---

31 *Seymour- An Introduction*, p109
32 *The Tower of Alchemy*, p38

180

ready, so I can be as absurd as God is."[33]

This point is summed up by G.K. Chesterton, describing the holy fool St. Francis of Assisi: "He had made a fool of himself... [T]here was not a rag of him that was not ridiculous. Everybody knew that at the best he had made a fool of himself. It was a solid objective fact, like the stones in the road, that he had made a fool of himself...[but] he was wearing the...word 'fool' as a feather in his cap; as a crest or crown. He would go on being a fool; he would become more and more of a fool; he would be the court fool of the King of Paradise. ...And we can say...that the stars which passed above... the rocky floor had for once in all their shining cycles round the world of laboring humanity, looked down upon a happy man."[34]

Ignorance is bliss. How perilously far we have come from wonder, exuberance, innocence, and laughter. And oh what foolishness it will require to take us back.

"You see, all of us go through the same doubts.
We are afraid of being mad; unfortunately for us, of course,
all of us are already mad."
don Juan[35]

Aleister Crowley furthers the idea that holiness and foolishness are one, stating: "The connection between foolishness and holiness is traditional. It is no sneer that the family nitwit had better go into the church. In the East the madman is believed to be 'possessed', a holy man or prophet. So

33 *Ecstasy*, p16,55
34 *St. Francis of Assisi*, p72,74,82
35 *Tales of Power*, p63. A Hindu verse runs: "Sometimes naked, sometimes mad, Now as a scholar, now as a fool, Thus they appear on earth- The free men!"

deep is this identity that it is actually embedded in the language. 'Silly' means empty- the Vacuum of Air- Zero-…And the word is from German *selig*, holy, blessed. It is the innocence of the Fool which most strongly characterizes him. …The Great Fool is definite doctrine. The world is always looking for a savior, and the doctrine in question is philosophically more than a doctrine; it is a plain fact."[36]

That is, the Pearl of Great Price, The Holy Grail, the Vision of God, Nirvana, Valhalla, Heaven, or Salvation, call it what you will, it will not be found until the individual forgets who they are, and what they are looking for. Then they shall find it. For, as Aleister Crowley relates: "Men smote me; then, perceiving that I was but a Pure Fool, they let me pass. Thus and not otherwise I came to the Temple of the Graal."[37]

*****

---

36 *The Book of Thoth*, p55

37 *Book of Lies*, p44. Shankara states of this type of liberated fool: "He may seem like a madman, or like a child, or sometimes like an unclean spirit. Thus he wanders the earth." (*Crest Jewel of Discrimination*, p111) And Sam Keen wrote: "To call a man a fool is not necessarily an insult, for the authentic life has frequently been pictured under the metaphor of the fool. In figures such as Socrates, Christ, and the Idiot of Dostoyevsky we see that foolishness and wisdom are not always what they seem to be. To the worldly-wise, the philosopher and the saint always appear foolish and incompetent." (*Apology for Wonder*, p128)

PART IV:
THE MYSTERY OF GOD

CHAPTER 11: The Highest Unknowable

"No matter what you touch and you wish to know about, you end up in a sea of mystery. ...it's like the essence, isn't that right, it remains. This is the greatest damn thing about the universe. That we can know so much, recognize so much, dissect, do everything, and we can't grasp it. And it's meant to be that way, do y'know. ... It's all mystery."
Henry Miller[1]

"...without even giving me time to know what it was called, I had somehow fallen down on my knees before it, like a slave I swear I don't know what had happened to me, but my heart was beating, I was I, and what had to happen was happening."
Clarice Lispector[2]

"I have sought for the geography of Nothingness, of unknown seas and another sun... for the rocking of a skeptical ocean in which islands and axioms are drowned, the vast liquid narcotic, tepid and sweet and tired of knowledge..."
E.M. Cioran[3]

"...mystery is quite another thing. ...to be in communion with that, the mind, the whole of you, must be at the same level, at the same time, with the same intensity as that which is called mysterious. This is love. With this the whole mystery of the universe is open."
Jiddu Krishnamurti[4]

---

1 *This is Henry, Henry Miller from Brooklyn*
2 *The Apple in the Dark*, p289
3 *A Short History of Decay*, p57
4 *Journal*, Apr 1975

This chapter begins the denouement of this investigation into ignorance, innocence, wonder, and mystery.

Here, at the threshold of unknowing all that is, we must prepare ourselves for another leap; which is to say, as before, we need to prepare ourselves to ...forget. For our purposes now, however, let us especially forget what we mean by the word God; that is, the instant the word God is used we must not know what that word means, for, as we shall see, the only way to know God ...is to not know God.

Recalling the chapter on 'the Virgin and the Child', it should be kept in mind that through the emptiness of innocence we give birth to another life; God emerges from the absence of any idea of God; it is from the inside-out, not from the outside-in, that God shall be Created, not found; which is to say, God comes out of one's ignorance, God does not go in through one's knowledge.

"But now you will ask me 'How am I to think of God himself, and what is he?' and I cannot answer you except to say 'I do not know!' For with this question you have brought me into the same darkness, the cloud of unknowing where I want you to be!"
The Cloud of Unknowing [5]

As it is perilous for us to have a single idea, concept, expectation, or speculation about any enigma whatsoever- for that destroys it's enigmaticism completely- it is of great importance that we admit once and for all that we do not understand the Great Enigma, God, and that perhaps we will

_____

5 p67

never know God, that God is categorically unknowable, and so we must release God from limitation, and let God be immense and unreachable.

> *"Can you simply agree that on some of the questions the mystery is too great ever for you to solve? Why not hold the mystery as sacred? And why not allow the sacred to be sacred, and leave it alone?"*
> God[6]

Can we not just leave *It* alone? Can we not just let God be God? Is it so hard to accept the impotence of our cognitive faculties, that we must continually desecrate that which is infinitely beyond our scope, by claiming to have even the slightest idea of what it is all about?

Let us remember the Fall, the reasons for it, and the way of return. "Mysteries are not to be solved", suggested Rumi, for "The eye goes blind/ when it only wants to see why."[7]

When we finally see mystery in all things- when we have stopped asking 'why?'- then we shall properly not know things. And when we do not know 'things', then we shall begin to see the one unknowable force in all things. And that unknowable force has, in the past, been called God. But, after all, God is just a word; it is a word for something we cannot understand.

"Brahma", says Shankara, "is indefinable, beyond the range of mind and speech..."[8]

Thus, by not-knowing, we have finally returned the

6 *Conversations with God*, by Neale Donald Walsch, p195
7 *The Essential Rumi*
8 *Crest Jewel of Discrimination*, p101

divine to unencumbered imagelessness; we return God to freedom by releasing God from the cages we have built. We have fulfilled the second commandment.[9]

> *"And if you would know God be not therefore*
> *a solver of riddles. "*
> Kahlil Gibran[10]

It is the same with God as with everything- there is no answer, no axiom, no truth, and no solution ...there is only riddle. There is only a solute called mystery, dis-solved in the solution called mystery. And that mystery has simply been named God. And "God is something that cannot be found by the mind", proclaimed Jiddu Krishnamurti.[11]

This is because the mind can 'know' only from one perspective, and yet it can 'unknow' from an infinity of implausible points of view; thus the *infinite* radiations of The Mystery of God are born in the spacious womb of this ignorance, and not in the confined ovum of conceptualization.

"If you are to know God divinely," intoned Meister Eckhart, "your own knowledge must become as pure ignorance, in which you forget yourself and every other creature."[12]

The Great Self (if I can use that term without muddling up our incomprehension) cannot be contained in the limited

---

9 "Make not unto thee any graven images..."
10 *The Prophet*
11 *Life Ahead*, chpt 7
12 Sermon 4. Let me digress a moment on the occasion of this last quote, and state that the verb 'to know' in old Hebrew, means both 'to understand', and 'to have intercourse with'. Thus, given the earlier findings in the chapter on 'The Virgin', we can see why Eckhart surmises that in order for us to 'know' god, we must 'become as pure ignorance', or, 'virginal', as it were, and then we shall have intimate inter-course or communion with the Unknowable.

vessel of the mind, and thus thought must be conquered, in order to let God be God.

The *kun byed rgyal po'i mdo*, speaking from the voice of the Creator, categorically states: "Oh great bodhisattva, listen! ...I do not teach that the objects are unrelated to the self because the root of all things is nothing but one self, and therefore it is impossible that the self looks at itself in terms of a doctrinal view. Therefore it is [known as] the teaching 'no contemplation of doctrinal views'. ...I transcend the scope of all sensory perception, and therefore from the primordial, there is no point in theorizing Me or in meditating upon Me. ...no doctrinal view [about Me] should be contemplated upon. Likewise...My true nature lack[s] meaning, so do not reflect upon a possible meaning. ... Unconceptualized I am beyond being an object of thinking. ...The nature of the All-Creating Sovereign, mind of perfect purity, is unborn and of a non-conceptual nature, and from it the various objects come forth as the wonders of origination...of ceaseless creation. ...Oh great bodhisattva, intuit this quintessential point! Because I am totally beyond the scope of sensory perception, I am beyond the scope of the senses, and I do not come through words. My nature is comprehensive and dwells in the empty circle. It is explained as non-conceptual, non-dual, and one from the primordial." [brackets are translator's][13]

Once again, it is absolutely ridiculous, and futile, to persist in trying to understand what cannot be understood; in our highest pursuits, the mind is absolutely not the Way, instead it is in the way.

M.L. Hawkins suggests to: "Go into the Darkness and put your hand into the hand of God. That shall be to you better than light and safer than a known way."

The 'infinite darkness', as stated by Hawkins above, is

---

13 p158,74,146,151,157,150

the mind's humble reckoning with the infinite enigma, and only from that humility is the truly magnificent seen for what it truly is: mind-boggling and ineffable. Only in the full appreciation and assimilation of this consciousness do we justify, and not blasphemy, the unsurpassable immensity of the unknowable word God.

"For it is man's function to contemplate the works of god;
and for this purpose was he made that he might view the
universe with wondering awe, and come to know its maker."
Hermetica.

The 'leap of faith' we have heard so much about is therefore not like some blind, cowardly hope directed towards the expectation that some outward, omnibenevolent force will intercede and protect us (which it might, though that is beyond what we're considering here), but faith, absolute faith, is the acceptance of walking with eyes fully open into the infinite darkness; faith is without expectation, hope, petition, or piety, or it is not faith, it is merely belief. Belief is a characteristic of concept, faith is a characteristic of mystery; for 'belief' is the acceptance of something we do not know, whereas 'faith' is the acceptance that we do not know.[14]

Therefore let us not belittle what is incomprehensible ...by claiming that we comprehend it. This is not simply my own little nudge in your ribs to 'give God his due', so to speak, it is actually of pragmatic importance so as to fully realize all that has been discussed here; for just as we can receive the knowable

---

14 Thankfully "Our understanding of the greatest matters will never be complete", Herakleitos reminds us. For, as Aleister Crowley succinctly puts it, "...the ultimate reason of things lies in a realm beyond manifestation and intellect." (*The Book of Thoth,* p82)

only by 'knowing', so it is that we can receive the Unknowable only by not-knowing.

"Truth comes to the thought of those who know him beyond thought, not to those who think it can be attained by thought. ...It is conceived of by him whom it is not conceived of; He by whom It is conceived of, knows it not. It is not understood by those who understand It. It is understood by those who understand it not."
Kena Upanishad

Seeking the Mystery of God is like seeking the mystery in all things- it is not so much a matter of seeking, but of a ubiquitous, unconditional, objectless, intelligent not-knowing. For the Unknowable is "Thou of whom no words can tell, no tongue can speak, whom silence only can declare", asserts the *Hermetica*.

Thus Elaine Pagels, author of *The Gnostic Gospels*, suggests, "...one cannot attain knowledge of the Unknown God. Any attempt to do so, to grasp the incomprehensible, hinders 'the effortlessness which is within you'."[15] Pagels then quotes from *Allogenes*, one of the codices from *The Nag Hammadi Library*, which runs: "...(whoever) sees (God) as he is in every respect, or would say that he is something like *gnosis* has sinned against him...because he did not know God."

Thus the true 'gnosis' of the Unknowable is actually 'agnosticism' in its most literal sense: a-gnosis, the absence of knowing.[16]

---

15 *The Gnostic Gospels*
16 Whitley Strieber states the paradox beautifully: "True agnosticism is a very active mental state, a sort of eager unknowing." (*Communion*, p278)

189

That is, when we unknow God and everything, then we will see God in everything, and we will not know what the word God means, and then we will know God.

Knowledge is necessarily relative. Only non-separative incomprehension can attain the Absolute.

"It is...clear", states Carl Jung, "that the God-image corresponds to a definite complex of psychological facts, and is thus a quantity which we can operate with; but what God is in himself remains a question outside the competence of all psychology. ...it must now be admitted that things exist in the psyche about which we know little or nothing at all...and that they possess at least as much reality as the things of the physical world which ultimately we do not understand either."[17]

"Whatsoever you can think about God is not going to be God; it is simply going to be thought."
Osho[18]

Following from this thought, Osho then suggested: "The ultimate is a mystery, then life becomes a life of wonder. ...And wherever you find mystery there is God. The more you know, the less you will be aware of God; the less you know, the closer God will be to you. If you don't know anything, if you say with absolute confidence 'I don't know' if this 'I don't know' comes from the deepest core of your being, then God will be in your very core, in the very beat of your heart. And then poetry arises...then one falls in love with this tremendous mystery that surrounds you."[19]

---

17 *Memories, Dreams, Reflections,* p65,165
18 *Book of Secrets*
19 *Ecstasy,* p15

Everyone must come to their own incomprehension of God their own way: whether it be from looking up at the night sky and witnessing the vast expanse of the unimaginably immense universe, or perhaps from viewing the marvels of the natural world, or mankind's mysterious ways, or by recognizing the inconceivable inward universe we all carry around with us. No matter how wonder comes, it matters only that we accept and revere it.

The authors of *The Kybalion* state: "The Hermetists believe and teach that THE ALL, 'in itself', is and must ever be UNKNOWABLE. They regard all the theories, guesses and speculations of the theologians and metaphysicians regarding the inner nature of THE ALL, as but the childish efforts of mortal minds to grasp the secret of the Infinite. Such efforts have always failed and will always fail, from the very nature of the task. One pursuing such inquiries travels around and around in the labyrinth of thought, until he is lost. He is like a squirrel which frantically runs around and around the circling treadmill wheel of his cage, travelling ever and yet reaching nowhere- at the end a prisoner still, and standing just where he started."[20]

Now, if we are reluctant to believe the adults who have been continuously quoted here, perhaps we should listen to what comes out of 'the mouths of babes', so to speak, and hear from a little girl named Anna. She says: "When you make Mister God really, really, really big, then you really, really, really, don't understand Mister God- then you do. ...Mister God keeps on shedding bits all the way through your life until the time comes when you admit freely and honestly that you don't understand Mister God at all. At this point you have let Mister God be his

---

20 p56. Addressing some such squirrels, one of Christ's disciples declared: "For as I was passing through and considering the objects of your worship, I even found an altar with this inscription: TO THE UNKOWN GOD. Therefore, the One whom you worship without knowing, Him I proclaim to you." (Acts 17:23)

proper size- and wham!- there he is, laughing at you."[21]

I suggest to anyone doubting the genius, and inherent spiritual vision of children, that they pick up the marvelous little book from which this last quote arises- *Mister God, This is Anna*- which is the true story of a four year old girl who was found abandoned on the docks in London, and who continually spouted the most profound and simple truths, exposing the imperfections of dogma and the availability of God to anyone open enough to allow the magnitude of the mystery of God in.

"Where he's concerned there are no boundaries.
You walk all your life, this one and the next, trying to reach
him, but the blessed fellow has no end."
Nikos Kazantzakis[22]

As we have seen, it is the original innocence (not original sin), and wondering vision of children that finds the ever-present connection with God, devoid of the hindrance of learned ideas, and the mist of rules.

This 'shedding bits', as little Anna called it, is the essence of the art of forgetting- the continual removing of obstacles until nothing is left. Sri Nisargaddata Maharaj furthers this 'shedding', stating: "Whoever goes there, disappears. It is unreachable by words, or mind. You may call it God, or *Parabrahman*, or Supreme Reality, but these are names given by the mind. It is the nameless, contentless, effortless and spontaneous state, beyond being and not being."[23]

Joel Goldsmith expands on this, stating: "No one is ever

---

21 from *Mister God, This is Anna*, by Fynn
22 *The Last Temptation of Christ*, p126
23 *I AM THAT*, p36

going to find God until he is stripped of all his concepts of God, until he leaves behind every synonym for God he has ever heard and launches forth into the unknown to discover the Unknowable. There is no such thing as a thought about God or a concept of God that is correct... Nothing we can think about God is truth; nothing we can read in a book about God is truth, because these represent merely limited human opinions about God."[24]

"There is nothing you can know about God that is God. There is no idea of God that you can entertain that is God. There is no possible thought that you can have about God that is God."
Joel Goldsmith[25]

Here we meet with Goldsmith's sedulous refusal to grant God any knowable attributes, which he so categorically assimilated into his occasional exegeses on Divine Unknowability.

Similarly, quoting an ancient hymn, Stepan Stulginsky writes: "Thou art One and in the secret of Thy unity the wisest of men are lost, because they know it not. ...Thou art existent; but the understanding and vision of mortals cannot attain to Thy existence, nor determine for Thee the Where, the How, and the Why. ...Thou art existent, and Thy existence is so profound and secret that none can penetrate and discover Thy secrecy."[26]

---

24 *The Art of Meditation*, p39
25 *The Contemplative Life*, p22. This uncompromising negationism is synopsized by Bede Griffiths, who declares of the Absolute: "It is 'unseen, inconceivable, unimaginable, indescribable'. Of every name and form which we may give to the supreme Being, we have to say: not this, not this- *neti, neti.*" (*The Marriage of East and West*, p17)
26 *Cosmic Legends of the East*, p7

Stulginsky then goes on to state: "In all legends and hymns it is pointed that an Omnipresent, Eternal, Boundless, and Immutable Principle transcends the power of human conception and could only be dwarfed by any human expression or similitude. Therefore it is considered that any reasoning about That is impossible... any judgements about That will inevitably be but a limitation of It. Grandeur and beauty of Infinity do not fit in our limited imagination or terms. They must stay in the limits of the ineffable. ...Let's find our place in the Great Cosmic Reality, which is not perverted with a mirage of the obviousity."[27]

Only the finite can be known, not the infinite; we may be able to identify certain aspects of the infinite, which are its finitudes, but that should not trick us into believing we know the whole of it. How could we? It is limitless. No matter how much we know (and we know very little) there is always a limitless amount we do not know, for even if we take away from infinity all that we know, there is no less of the infinity that we still do not know (i.e. $\infty - 1 = \infty$).

Hence reductionism (by which I mean reason, logic, or the knowing of 'separate' things) must necessarily fail to grasp the full picture, for, as we all know from the study of complete systems, as stated earlier: the whole is greater than the sum of the parts. Therefore we cannot look at a piece of the puzzle and claim to understand the puzzle; we must look not at the parts and say "these are only parts" we must look at the parts and say "there are no parts", there is only an unknowable whole.

The realization of this would lead Goldsmith into a

---

27 *Cosmic Legends of the East*, p88. This is the same realization that would bring the great modern logician, Ludwig Wittgenstein, to finish his brutally recondite work, *Tractatus Logico-Philosophicus*, with the humbling and contradictory acknowledgement that his real argument was an argument against itself. He wrote: "My propositions are elucidatory in this way: he who understands me finally recognizes them as senseless, when he has climbed out through them, on them, over them... He must surmount these propositions; then he sees the world rightly. [For] whereof one cannot speak, thereof one must be silent." (sections 6.54-7)

respectable attempt at defining what in fact cannot be defined. He offers: "When every concept had been brushed aside, I was left with the term 'the Infinite Invisible'. Why 'the Infinite Invisible?' Because the Infinite Invisible did not mean anything that I could understand. Neither you nor I can grasp the Infinite; neither you nor I can see the Invisible. The Infinite Invisible is a term that denotes something which cannot be comprehended by the finite mind. That does not mean, however, that the Infinite Invisible is the correct term for God. It is correct for me, because it provides me with a term which my mind can encompass. That satisfies me. If I could grasp the meaning of the Infinite Invisible, it would be within range of my human comprehension, and I do not want that kind of God."[28]

> *"He, the Self, is to be described as No, no!*
> *He is incomprehensible, for he cannot be comprehended."*
> Khandogya Upanishad

It is only necessary, then, for us to relinquish our singular perspectives and embrace instead the 'whole' as the mystery which it is, by acknowledging that we perceive only within the limitedness of our 'place' or 'context' within the whole; which is to say, we cannot understand the whole, for 'all is One', and this 'One' is so incredibly huge that only a mind which perceives everything at once could understand everything, and since our minds do not encompass the all, we perceive partially, not impartially. It is in recognizing these blinders- that we can see very little of the immense magnitude of the all- that we allow the infinite mystery to exist behind them. The Mystery is One Huge Mystery. Let our actions and understandings be

---

28 *Way of Meditation*, p40

founded upon this antecedent. For if we do not perceive *in toto*, and we do not, we simply re-ceive a part. Impartiality, then, is the acceptance of our limitation within limitlessness; it is accepting that the whole is unknown by us, and therefore every partial perspective is suspect of fraud.

When we have given God back his or her rightful being- which is to say, his or her unknowability- then what happens is that we begin to also find out our own proper place in the cosmos; when the event (God) which is so important to our lives becomes impossible to understand, then we also become impossible to understand, after all we were 'created in his own image'. And if that image is beyond our imagination, then we must also be beyond our own imagination.

> *"Once His attributes are exhausted, no one will have the energy to forge Him new ones; and the creature having assumed, then rejected, them will go and rejoin in nothingness, his loftiest invention: his Creator."*
> E.M. Cioran[29]

When God's attributes are gone, our own attributes are gone, and only then is it possible for the two mysteries to blend into One; before this absolute unknowing occurred- when we 'knew' God and ourselves- we saw them as distinct, different entities- for that was the only way to 'know' them (i.e. by separating them), but when we finally 'unknow' God and ourselves, only then, when the lines of division vanish, can the separate entities merge into One.

Henry Miller described this confluence, with a description of Proust's inner struggle, when he wrote: "It was a

---

29 *A Short History of Decay*, p138

return to the labyrinth, a desire to bury himself deeper and deeper in the self. And this self was for him composed of a thousand different entities all attached by experience to a mysterious seed-like Self which he refused to know."[30]

Thus anything we say or write about the 'great unknowable', which is life, is incorrect. In the attempt to define life in any way, we steal its beauty from ourselves.

For, in fact, mystery preceded God. Hence June Singer asserts: "There is One, beyond Jehovah, beyond Elohim, beyond all knowing, whose nature may be contemplated but not grasped. ...[For] before there was matter or any created thing, or any Creator to conceive of creation; before all that, there was Mystery."[31]

In the beginning was Mystery.

At the quintessential point of openness- when the conditioned mind forgets itself completely- that is when the little being ends, judgement ceases, and the great emptiness occurs which encompasses everything completely; at this point, where duality dissolves away, Jiddu Krishnamurti would say, "the observer is the observed"; a classical Hindu saint would say- "I am That"; in colloquial terms we would simply state, "I am the all and the everything"; And Christ would say, "I and the Father are One". For at this point God now recognizes Him or Herself in you, and as you, and as the Creator of all that is Created, which is naught but God at every moment, living in and as the Mystery of Godness.

But perhaps we have arrived at this supposition too quickly, and have jumped briefly into the topical agenda of the final chapter. Let us go no further than to finish with a few more quick sorties into the future. Let us re-enter the Garden, let us stay there.

---

30 *Wisdom of the Heart*, p167
31 *Androgyny*, p91,152

*"When we walk to the edge of all the light we have and take the
step into the darkness of the unknown we must believe one of
two things will happen- there will be something solid for us to
stand on, or we will be taught how to fly."*
Claire Morris[32]

And, more importantly, as we shall see in a very short
time, when we leap off into the unknown, we ...become one with
the unknown. That is: "Man is My mystery, and I am his
mystery...", stated Baha'u'llah, in the *Kitab-i-lquan*.[33]

All is one mystery, we need only recognize this, and be
it. Realizing this, Clarice Lispector stated of one of her
characters: "Because in one perfect moment the world had
become whole again, even with its ancient mystery- except that
this time, before the enigma had closed...[she] had put herself
inside of it, just as enigmatic as the enigma."[34]

*****

32 *The Haven Book*, from Gabriola Island
33 *Kitab-i-lquan*, p65
34 *The Apple in the Dark*, p172

CHAPTER 12: The Immanence of Wonder

"...what happened to me is- I became an angel."
       Henry Miller[1]

"There's a place where, before order and names, I am I!"
       Clarice Lispector[2]

"If with each word we win a victory over nothingness, it is only better to endure its reign. We die in proportion to the words which we fling around us. ...Those who speak have no secrets. And we all speak. We betray ourselves... executioner of the unspeakable, each of us labors to destroy all the mysteries, beginning with our own."
       E.M. Cioran[3]

"I am sorrow, pain, and fleeting pleasure; the passions and the gratifications; the bitter wrath and infinite compassion; the sin and the sinner. I am the lover and the very love itself. I am the saint, the adorer, the worshipper, and the follower. I am God."
       Jiddu Krishnamurti[4]

1 *Tropic of Capricorn*
2 *The Apple in the Dark*, p345
3 *A Short History of Decay*, p17
4 *The Path*

When we have come to see everything as mystery, including ourselves, and we have come to know that God is the one mystery which is everything, then we shall come to realize that ...*we are the mystery which is God*; that is, having forgotten what we thought we knew, and what we think we are, we find that we exist wholly ensconced in the one-limitless-enigma, and, in fact, not only are we in that enigma, but we actually *are* The Enigma. And that Enigma, for a great part of history, has been called God. We are Mystery. We are God.

Ah, but wait a minute, how is that possible? How could we be both ignorant *and* God at the same time? And the answer, as we shall see in the following pages, is: nobody knows (not even God).

But first, regarding the immanent nature of Mystery- the fact that we are the greatest of wonders to ourselves- Joseph Campbell states: "Not the animal world, nor the plant world, nor the miracle of the spheres, but man himself is now the crucial mystery". And Lindsay Clarke's character proffers, "It's my contention that there are mysteries enough in here [tapping at his breast] to keep a man occupied without meddling in foreign parts."[5]

"When we think of that sense and that feeling, or that inclination, which makes us affirm the word 'I', it is difficult to point out what it is, what is its character; for it is something which is beyond human comprehension."
Hazrat Inayat Kahn[6]

---

5 *Chymical Wedding*, p35. St. Augustine stated: "Men go abroad to wonder at the height of mountains, at the huge waves of the sea, at the long courses of the rivers, at the vast compass of the oceans, at the circular motions of the stars, and they pass by themselves without wondering."
6 *The Mysticism of Music, Sound, and Word*, p246

The mystery is in us. Wonder lies within; God, or Heaven, or the 'Kingdom of Spirit', call it what you will, it is that which lies nowhere but inside us.

Alipi announced: "...if that which thou seekest thou find not within thee, thou wilt never find it without thee. If thou knowest not the excellency of thine own house, why dost thou seek and search after the excellency of other things? The universal Orb of the world contains not so many great mysteries and excellencies as a little Man, formed by God in His image. And he who desirest the primacy among the students of Nature will nowhere find a greater or better field of study than himself."[7]

"It is the study of self which is really the study of God. ...[And] every soul has in himself a Kingdom of God. To become conscious of this mystery of life is to open one's eyes to the kingdom of God."
Kahn[8]

Absolute wonderment, then, is simply a person's realized relationship to a suddenly recognized unfathomableness- their own unfathomable Self.

As John Claypool remarks, "Several years ago I came across the phrase, 'the mystery that is every man.' From the moment I saw it I liked it, because it reminds me of a fact about every person who has ever lived- that everyone is a dynamic,

---

7 *The Salt of Nature Regenerated*
8 *The Mysticism of Music, Sound, and Word*, p127,225

mysterious reality..."[9]

All we need to do is be aware of ourselves completely; to be 'open' and not closed off by preconceptions or desires about who we are or want to be. We must simply *be*, and finally we shall see ourselves truly- as miracles now and always.

It is only through our de-finitions of ourselves that we become finite, definable fragments, separated from the glorious One. By undefining ourselves and everything, we then become intimate with, and not separate from, the unfathomable whole.

> *"We wake, if ever we wake at all, to mystery."*
> Annie Dillard[10]

We wake *as* mystery.

"For where, indeed, could 'the Mystery' be more cleverly hidden", asked Alan Watts, "than right in the seeking and the seeker...?"

It is not the world which is astounding, it is the 'I'; the astounding *is* the astounded; that 'I am!', *is* the wonder of wonders.

Kahn declares, "Man is a mystery in all aspects of his being; not only in mind and soul, but also in that organism which he calls his body. ...And so it is with the man who seeks the mystery of life outside; he will never find it, for the mystery of life is only to be found within."[11]

---

9 *The Light Within You*, p83. That is: "We live on the edge of the miraculous all our lives", adds Miller, and, "The miracle is in us, and it blossoms forth the moment we lay ourselves open to it." (*The Absolute Collective*)

10 *Pilgrim at Tinker Creek*, p2

11 *The Mysticism of Music, Sound, and Word*, p158,162. And from Whitley Strieber: "I am not the only mystery walking this earth. Everyone of us is a mystery. We do not know who we are, not one of us." (*Transformation*, p115)

Who am I? What am I? Why am I? Are these questions not the very basis of our beings? Are we not, in fact, wholly unanswerable questions? Are we not *the* mystery, awakening to itself?

Ernest Becker commented: "Man's very insides- his self- are foreign to him. He doesn't know who he is, why he was born, what he is doing on the planet, what he is supposed to do, what he can expect. His own existence is incomprehensible to him, a miracle just like the rest of creation, closer to him, right near his pounding heart, but for that reason all the more strange."[12]

Indeed, what we must look upon with most catholicity- what we must lose all memory of, what we must perceive with no preconceptions whatsoever- is not the strange and impressive world outside of us, but instead what lies 'right inside our breast', which is to say, ourselves, our 'I'- the Mystery incarnate within, and as, each one of us.

Lispector described this necessary completion in one of her characters, writing: "[He] had fallen so deep into himself that he could not recognize himself. ...[And so] accepting was accepting a great and obscure meaning that came from meeting with the unknown creature that he was."[13]

We see now that wonder is not in the world, it is in mankind. 'Exasperation' occurs not as a function of any particular event but as the capability of the individual to be exasperated, to *be* exasperation. Awe is simply the flagship of perspectives, not that we have but ...that we are; exasperation is not a sense of being, it is being; one *is* exasperation. The person who is aghast, is aghastness aghast at itself.[14]

---

12 *The Denial of Death*, p51
13 *The Apple in the Dark*, p231,239
14 Gabriel Marcel noted: "A mystery is something in which I am myself involved, and it can therefore only be thought of as a sphere where the distinction between what is in me and what is before me loses its meaning and its initial distinction." (*Being and Having*,

*"Remember that in pure…mind essence there is no asking of
the question why and not even any significance attached to it.
…Why don't you just relax and enjoy God?
God is you, you fool!"*
Jack Kerouac[15]

We are the center of a vastness that has no limitation; we
cannot get closer to the mystery of God than in ourselves. We
must not look for the mystery outside of ourselves, for it is not
outside; we must recognize ourselves as Mystery, emanating
mysteriously, from our own mysteriousness.

In Baha'u'llah's prophetic words, "Know, verily, that
the soul is a sign of God, a heavenly gem whose reality the most
learned of men hath failed to grasp, and whose mystery no mind,
however acute, can ever hope to unravel."[16]

As such, Osho claimed: "God has already happened.
You are carrying him from the very beginning... You may have
forgotten, you may have become completely oblivious, you may
not be able to remember who you are, but still you are God."[17]

Life is all one great event not understanding itself. And
we are IT, not understanding Itself. We are the 'I' which does
not know what 'I' is.[18]

Indeed it is an absolute tragedy that we spend our days
hunting for spectacle and distraction, when the most marvelous,

---

p117)

15 *Dharma Bums*, p202,111

16 *Gleanings from the Writings of Baha'u'llah*, section lxxxii

17 *Ecstasy*, p21

18 "Western humans have lost their sense of unity with the cosmos", claimed the
unprecedented brother duo of Terrence and Dennis McKenna, "and with the transcendent
mystery within themselves."

intimate miracle lies right inside of us, and is us; for when we see and seek outwardly with only our own limited perspective, God the Great Mystery shrinks into an ungreat unmystery within us.

"By dint of accumulating non-mysteries and monopolizing non-meanings, life inspires more dread than death: it is life which is the Great Unknown."
E.M. Cioran[19]

We are Life. We are not outside of it. What we are, it is.

We have been on the shore of 'knowing' too long. It is high time for us to leap into the river of unknowing, and let the miracle of god flow through us, and as us, for, as Thomas Jeffers pronounces, "...'God' will be unseeing as well as unseen till he has an 'I' who can watch and act for him."[20]

As well, the *kun byed rgyal po'i mdo*, again in the voice of the Creator, states: "Oh great bodhisattva, listen! [My] own being [even] in its variety is not two, but also each part in itself is not...conceptualizable. ...I Myself, the All-Creating Sovereign, teach My own being after I caused it to become apparent. ...The individual actuation lets you see the whole. In such a way My own being is also taught. ...If I, the All-Creating, am not met then all...beings living in this...world will not understand their own being nor their actuating force. ...Therefore they will not see that I, the All-Creating Sovereign and their own being are not different. ...For this reason, you must teach My own being."[21]

It is we who must return God's own vision to the

19 *A Short History of Decay*, p10
20 *Samuel Butler Revalued*, p92. Similarly Mike Stack exclaims of this mutual dependency, "It is a philosophical nightmare- IT only sees what I know."
21 p122,91,161,132

wonders of God. Such was the realization that would lead Kazantzakis to put the following words into the mouth of Christ: "This was...a good moment to reveal the word which the Lord confided in me and to awaken the God that sleeps within these men and women who destroy themselves in the pursuit of vain cares... [For] great things happen when God mixes with man. Without man, God would have no mind on this earth to reflect upon his creatures intelligibly..."[22]

To become conscious of our own mysteriousness, is to become conscious of God's mysteriousness, for there is no difference. All is mystery.

**"The presence of God is within our Consciousness.
The nature of God is I."**
Joel Goldsmith[23]

'I' is the substance of God; individuals are merely the forms that 'I' takes.

To better recognize this, Shankara explains why our 'I' is God's 'I'; he states: "A jar made of clay is not other than clay. It is clay essentially. The form of the jar has no independent existence. What then, is the jar? Merely an invented name! The form of the jar can never be perceived apart from the clay. What, then, is the jar? An appearance! The reality is the clay itself."[24]

The Self is all selves; the mysteries are One mystery.

Our 'I' has been God all along. But how could we not

---

22 *The Last Temptation of Christ*, p265,274. As such Jung adds, "That is the meaning of divine service, of the service which man can render to God, that light may emerge from the darkness, that the Creator may become conscious of His creation, and man conscious of himself." *Memories, Dreams, Reflections*, p338
23 *Way of Meditation*, p42
24 *Crest Jewel of Discrimination*, p67

have known that? It is absurd that God should not understand God. And yet ...how else explain the unexplainable? Everything is God, but no one knows what God is, not even God.

Perhaps, in fact, this absurdity was the intent all along- to be so mysterious that we could not recognize ourselves as we truly are, and the whole game of being (if 'game' is the appropriate word for this implausible tangle) was, and is, to grope and grope through the dark of the self, until IT finally figures Itself out.

Neale Donald Walsch quotes God as stating: "Since it is the greatest desire of the soul (God) to experience Itself as the Creator ...We had no choice other than to find a way to forget all about Our creation."(brackets are author's)[25] Note that this statement comes right from the horse's mouth, so to speak.

The assumption here is that at some point in our spiritual evolution we had to forget our true selves- our Creator selves- for this was the only way God could play hide-and-seek inside his or her own creation. This is the same old wearisome story, recounted every now and then by anyone brave or crazy enough to imagine it, about how God became bored of being alone and omniscient, and so had to differentiate and hide within His own creation in order to experience the joy of rediscovering himself.

Neale Donald Walsch, author of *Conversations With God*, responds to the last statement by God, questioning: "I am amazed that we found a way. Trying to 'forget' that we are all One, and that the One of which we are is God, must be like trying to forget that a pink elephant is in the room. How could we be so mesmerized?"[26]

Well, we did indeed forget. And now the horrible truth is that we must forget ourselves again; we must forget our false selves in order to remember our true selves.

---

25 *Conversations with God Vol III*, p53
26 *ibid.*

"The goal of self-consciousness is to find oneself, this being the finding of God. It is as though God in his known capacity hid himself... allowing mankind to progress in an independent manner."
Eom Ida Mingle[27]

Similarly, the idiosyncratic thinker, Neville, states: "Deliberately, [God] has become man and has forgotten that He is God, in the hope that man, thus Created, will eventually rise as God. ...[For] just as God in His love for man so completely identified Himself with man that He forgot that He was God, so man in his love for God must so completely identify himself with God that he lives the life of God."[28]

The mystery of God lies within us; we *are* the narrow gate, but we have forgotten that the password to the mystery is 'I'.

Of this, Alan Watts wrote: "...this is the dramatic image of Brahma playing hide-and-seek with himself through all the ages of time, concealing himself with infinite ingenuity in the endless variety of apparently separate forms and beings, throwing himself away to recover himself with ever renewed surprise, plunging into ever more fantastically lost situations so that the finding again is all the more astounding. ...[This is the] Hindu concept of *maya*- the dramatic self-deception whereby the One plays at being the Many, and the Godhead lets itself be forgotten in pretending to be each individual being."[29]

---

27 *The Science of Love*, p179. Maitreya Ishwara comments that "...[life] is a divine play of hide and seek. God hides and you seek... you are a part of God lost in samsara...[but someday] you [will] fully reunite with That, the unknowable mystery of non-Being."
28 *The Law and the Promise*, p147
29 *The Two Hands of God*, p32,42. Swamiji asserts: "...there is a possibility for you to

Life is a ruleless game, played by a multifarious cast of individuals who are not individual, but are God not knowing it is play.

The anonymous writer of *The Way Beyond* explains: "We have called It the Higher Self, and it is in fact [the] very *God in you*. It is like a ray or reflection of God's mind shining somewhere deep within your consciousness- a 'light which shineth in the darkness, but the darkness (of the outer human mind) knoweth it not.' For certainly when It can get your mind's attention and you listen, It displays a wisdom that is near to that God as the human mind can conceive. And those who heed and obey are given a glimpse of something wonderful, which while inexpressible is altogether divine and most satisfying. ...Everyone must come to that place- every seeker of the true way of life; for until self with its human mind has been completely humbled and gives up utterly, it cannot accept the truth of its non-reality and of the actuality of the God-man within..." (brackets are author's)[30]

"You are the meaning deepest inside things,
that never reveals the secret of its owner."
Rainer Maria Rilke[31]

---

stay aloof from this intellect and not to worry about evolution because you are the free Being who, in the beginning, was never bound until it manifested the conscious aspect and became the intellect. The basic idea is that you don't need to meditate because you are a free Being. ...My information is that you are capable, without meditating, of knowing that whom you call I, the life, the Being, is forever free and is never modified into any thing or any relation. It is not tagged to the body, intellect, or ideas. It is forever free. But it has the capacity to release a power out of itself and continue to lay a trip on the body level, calling itself bound and wondering how to be free. That is the play of Being." (Talks, Dec. 1998)

30 *The Way Beyond*, p58
31 *You are the Future*

It is becoming apparent why life is the outlandish absurdity which it is- because the Unknowable Creator is caught in an unknowable creation and is trying to use knowing as a way to get out.

This concept is advanced in *The Kybalion* of hermetic philosophy, which runs as follows: "This process is called the stage of Involution, in which THE ALL becomes 'involved', or 'wrapped up', in its creation. This process is believed by the Hermeticists to have a Correspondence to the mental process of an artist, writer, or inventor, who becomes so wrapped up in his mental creation as to almost forget his own existence and who, for the time being, almost 'lives in his creation'. If instead of 'wrapped' we use the word 'rapt', perhaps we will give a better idea of what is meant."[32]

Now, summarizing the absurdity of this immanent show, Elsa Barker relates the words of an anonymous spirit in *Letters from a Living Dead Man*, which state: "Sometimes when praying, for I prayed much, there would come to me the sudden question, 'To what are you praying?' And I would answer aloud, 'To God, to God!' But though I prayed to Him everyday for years, only occasionally did I get a flash of that true consciousness of God. Finally one day when I was alone in the woods, there came the great revelation. It came not in any form of words, but rather in a wordless and formless wonder, too vast for the limitation of thought. ...Then gradually...I could put into the form of words the realization which had been too much for my mortality to bear, and the words I used to myself were, 'All that is, is God.' It seemed very simple, yet it was far from simple. 'All that is, is God.' That must include me and my fellow beings... From that moment life assumed a new meaning for me. I could not see a human face without remembering the

---

32 *The Kybalion*, p102

revelation- that the human being I saw was a part of God. ...The realization nearly took my breath away. Life became unbelievably beautiful. ...[For] I found that as more and more I sought God in [others], more and more God responded to me through them. And life became still more wonderful. ...Sometimes I tried to tell others what I felt, but they did not always understand me. It was thus I began to realize that God had purposely, for some reason of his own, covered Himself with veils. Was it that He might have the pleasure of tearing them away?"[33]

God wakes up to Godness with bewildered astonishment.[34]

"We do not even know what the self is."
Swamiji Shyam[35]

Therefore, if we are to alter the game, we must simply cease being suffering, separate, created beings, and instead return to the memory of the enigmatic One Being which we have for too long fallen away from, through the infinite labyrinths of our own Godlike amnesia, as it were.

As Meister Eckhart declared: "He, then, who is to be poor in spirit must be poor of all his own knowledge, so that he knows nothing of God, or creatures, or of himself. ...For if God once found a person as poor as this, he would take the responsibility of his own action and would himself be the scene of action, for God is one who acts within himself. It is here, in

---

33 *Letters from a Living Dead Man*, p80-82
34 "I hear and behold God in every object, yet I under-/stand God not in the least,/Nor do I understand who there can be more wonder-/Ful than myself." Walt Whitman (*Leaves of Grass*)
35 Talks, Mar 1999

211

this poverty, that man regains the eternal being that once he was, now is, and evermore shall be."[36]

Eckhart is saying that once we become empty of all the dross within, God the Mystery can do nothing but rush in to fill the vacuum of our absence.

It is up to each one of us to choose between suffocating in the vortex of the limited, knowable self, or instead to cut the cords which bind, and let ourselves drift out into, and *be*, the vast, incomprehensible sea of Being itself.[37]

"My plan, then, in so far as the negation of all effort and purpose may be said to be a plan, is to stop evolving, to remain what I am and to become more and more only what I am- that is, to become more miraculous."
Henry Miller[38]

To 'become more and more' ourselves, is to become freer, more Unknowable, more Godlike, more and more The Great Sea of Mystery that is contained in every part of that

---

36 sermon 28

37 Joseph Campbell states that the mystical function in humans is designed "...to awaken and maintain in the individual a sense of awe and gratitude in relation to the mystery dimension of the universe, not so that he lives in fear of it, but so that he recognizes that he participates in it, since the mystery of being is the mystery of his own deep being as well." Thus, "In the orient the ultimate divine mystery is sought beyond all human categories of thought and feeling, beyond names and forms...[and] is to be realised as the ground of one's own very being. ...That is the realisation formulated in those famous words of the gentle Brahmin Aruni to his son, recorded in the *Chhandogya Upanishad* of about the eighth century B.C.: 'You, my dear Shivetaketu, you are It'- *tat tvam asi*. ...Only when that mortal 'you' will have erased everything about itself that it cherishes and is holding to, will 'you' have come to the brink of an experience of identity with that Being which is no being yet is the Being beyond the nonbeing of all things." (*Myths to Live By*, p221,94)

38 *Hamlet Letters*. As such Austin Osman Spare stoically declared: "Know my purpose: To be a stranger unto myself, the enemy of truth."

Mystery called 'I'.

Dag Hammarskjold asserted this when he wrote: "At every moment you choose yourself, but do you choose your self? Body and soul contain a thousand possibilities out of which you may build many 'I's'. But in only one of them is there congruence between the elector and the elected, only one which you will never find until you have excluded all those superficial feelings and possibilities with which you toy out of curiosity or wonder or fear and which hinder you from casting anchor in the experience in the mystery of life and the consciousness of the talent entrusted in you and the wonder of you which is your 'I'."

If we seek to understand life (the life which we are), we will never see it as it is- i.e. not understandable. However, if we give ourselves away, forget everything, and open up to the grand possibility that we are limitless, then, and only then, will the unfathomable, blissful mystery which we are dance naked right before us.

Zen Master Yuansou asserts: "This inconceivable door of great liberation is in everyone. It has never been blocked, it has never been defective. Buddhas and Zen masters have appeared in the world and provided expedient methods, with many different devices, using illusory medicines to cure illusory illnesses, just because your faculties are unequal, your knowledge is unclear, you do not transcend what you see...and you are tumbled about endlessly in an ocean of misery by afflictions due to ignorance, by emotional views and habitual conceptions of others and self, right and wrong. The various teachings and techniques of Buddhas and Zen masters are only set forth so that you will individually step back into yourself, understand your own original mind and see your own original nature..."[39]

Here we are reminded of our 'original' nature, which is

---

39 *Zen Essence*, p78

pristine, untainted, virginal, knowledgeless nature.

With this in mind, Lispector wrote about one of her characters, stating: "But after ignoring the lesser truths, he began to resemble other beings, as if enshrouded in mystery. His ignorance transformed him into a mysterious being."[40]

"'I am that I am' is what every sacred being seems to say.
...[And] the response of the imagination
to such a presence or significance is a passion of awe."
Keats

And so the absence of rapture exists only because we imagine ourselves as separate, suffering, detached, and limited beings, and therefore 'outside' the fullness of the One Mystery called God, the Self, the Source, or what have you.

An anonymous anecdote from the East will further support this point:

"Master" said the student "where do you get your spiritual power?"
"From being connected to the source," said the Master.
"You are connected to the source of Zen?"
"Beyond that," said the Master, "I am Zen. The connection is complete."
"But isn't it arrogant to claim connection with the source?" asked the student.
"Far from it," said the Master. "It's arrogant not to claim connection with the source. Everything is connected. If you think you are not connected to the source you are thumbing your nose at the universe itself."

---

40 *Jorno do Brasil*, Nov 13/71

The lesson is simple- We are the Source. We are the Creators. We are the all and the everything. We are God.

The absurd thing about this, however, is that ...God does not understand how it is possible; *God is a mystery to God.*[41]

If, after all, it is true that 'God' is what cannot be understood, then if a person thinks they understand God, it is not really God that they understand. For a God which is not a mystery, is not God.

'God', in fact, is the only word that properly expresses our non-understanding of things; 'God' is the window to the abyss- the word that opens every wordless door, as long as we consciously do not know what lies on the other side.

"God is never an explanation.
It is the most profound and utter declaration of 'I don't know'
and yet in this unknowing lies the I AM."
Richard Moss[42]

This realization is further described in a short anecdote by the anonymous spirit in *Letters from a Living Dead Man*. He relates: "There is a mystery here which I cannot fathom. ...One night I seemed to be reclining on a moonbeam, which means that the poet which dwells in all men was awake in me. I seemed to be reclining upon a moonbeam, and ecstasy filled my heart. For the moment I had escaped the clutches of Time, and was living

---

41 "We all agree that your theory is crazy, but is it crazy enough?" (Niels Bohr to Wolfgang Pauli)

42 *The Black Butterfly*, p77. Chokecherry Gall Eagle similarly relates: "...one of the greatest things is that we can re-enter this touching of Holiness of Life, this Great Holy Spirit in all things, including in us. This is healing. It is the true healing that counts. To me: *It is the wonder and awe of Life.*" (*Beyond the Lodge of the Sun*, p163)

in that etheric quietude which is merely the activity of rapture raised to the last degree. I must have been enjoying a foretaste of that paradoxical state which the wise ones of the East call Nirvana. ...I was vividly conscious of the moonbeam and of myself, and *in* myself seemed to be everything else in the universe. It was the nearest I ever came to a realization of that supreme declaration, 'I am' ...[Though] I marvelled not, because the state of my consciousness *was* marvel."[43]

We are all 'I's'. Everything is I, Everything is marvel, and mystery. What we claim to know as separate things, or even separate Mysteries, are unseparate parts of the Whole. So we can only become contiguous with the One Mystery by recognizing the Mystery within each one of us, which we are, which we call 'I'.

To become exasperated by the implausibility of our own existence, is to become the implausibility of existence. Which is to say, it is to become existence.

"The truth is always some inner power without explanation. The more genuine part of my life is unrecognizable, extremely intimate and impossible to define. ...I am so mysterious that I do not understand myself."
Clarice Lispector[44]

It is in the relinquishing of personal attributes, definitions, and expectations that the event which we are is laid bare before us.

Ernest Becker stated: "Out of the ruins of the broken cultural self there remains the mystery of the private invisible,

---

43 *Letters from a Living Dead Man*, p167-169
44 *The Hour of the Star*, p12. *JdoB*, 1968

inner self which yearned for ultimate significance... The invisible mystery at the heart of every creature now attains cosmic significance by affirming its connection with the invisible mystery at the heart of creation."[45]

That is, when we recognize our own mysteriousness, we become one with the mysterious universe. And along these lines, Rabidrinath Tagore offered: "The traveler has to knock at every alien door to come to his own, and one has to wander through all the outer worlds to reach the innermost shrine at the end...[and then] melt into tears of a thousand streams and deluge the world with the flood of the assurance 'I am!'"[46]

Thus Ramtha was able to find God and himself as the very same self. He offers: "...that which I was going to, which was *my* home, was the great, elusive Unknown God, the grand mystery that caused all things to occur. ...[But] who was the Unknown God? It was me... My path in my life was to become the Unknown God- which, I was to discover, was myself- and to go beyond the dimensions to frolic in the adventures of forever. ...[Know that] you *are* God. You always have been, you always will be...[and] this grand understanding...you *allowed* to be taken away from you. And [so] from every adventure along the way, you will gain a greater perception of the mystery of yourself. ...then you can say with grace, dignity, and humble strength...the I AM that I am is the essence of All That Is. ...To become God is to say...'I Am' ...[For] you are gods created of God...gods living in the wonderment of their own creation. "[47]

Indeed, the mystery of the 'I' inside of us is the mystery

---

45 *The Denial of Death*, p91
46 *Gitanjali*, XII
47 *Ramtha*, p23,210,102,14. The mystery of the 'I AM' arises from the great tradition of Yahweh's definition of himself- "I am that I am", and Christ's timeless phrase- "Before Abraham was, I AM". It is also expressed by Lispector, as, "I am, therefore, I am." (*JdoB*, 1968), and is conveyed still more succinctly by Swamiji Shyam, who says simply, "I am I".

of God, for "the kingdom of God lies within", as you will recall. It is only when we give up the preconceptions we have of ourselves that we open up to the Great Mystery which is in us, which is 'I', which is God. For, just as God cannot be known by the mind, neither can 'I'.

All is One Mystery. There is no division. We are all the One God Mystery, and yet God cannot even understand how that is possible.[48]

"You are what you can't find."
Tigger, from Winnie-the-Pooh

Which is to say, the Self cannot be known to itself, for it is indefinable, acontextual, and infinite. Only that which is finite can be de-fined.[49]

On this point Lao Tzu suggested, "It is called mystery. Meet it, you cannot see its face; follow it, you cannot see its back."

And the *kun byed rgyal po'i mdo* states: "A contemplation of the great good qualities cannot be achieved through contemplating them by means of contemplation itself. ...Likewise, the immutable mind, this very mind itself, cannot be realized through one's own mind. ...Consequently, the pristine awareness cannot be object to the pristine awareness."[50]

---

48 In the 'channeled' book, *Original Cause*, the voice of God declares: "I am, but what am I, who am I, where am I, and what does it mean to be?" (received by Ceanne DeRohan, p3)

49 From the *Corona Class Lessons*, Kuthumi admonishes: "The frailty of human reason is ever in its identification with the finite self. A sense of being entangled in the processes of identification with objects and experiences hinders the revelation of man's true spiritual nature. ...[For] God is not the mind that comprehends and knows in part." (p259-260)

50 p119,115,159. Rene Guenon, commenting on the *Kena Upanishad*, writes "It is the

What these differing quotes are saying is that we cannot 'know' our 'I' directly.

Jean Paul Sartre describes this as such: "The very meaning of knowledge is what it is not and is not what it is; for in order to know being such as it is, it would be necessary to be that being. But there is this 'such as it is' only because I am not the being which I know..."[51]

Another way of looking at it is this: when the little self dissolves in the big Self, every division ends; subject and object become one. As such the mystery and the perceiver of the mystery are no longer separate. Thus knowledge- which is an event that exists only when the One is divided into the 'ten thousand things'- ends, and so the knower ends with the knowledge. Everything becomes mystery.

"When, having thought of everything, he thinks of himself- for he manages this only by the detour of the universe, as if he were the last problem he proposes to himself- he remains astonished, confused..."
E.M. Cioran[52]

In Osho's words: "Knowledge is a bridge between the object and the subject. If they are not separate, the bridge cannot exist. ...We are one with it, there is no space between us and the truth, so we cannot become the knower."[53]

Knower, and the Knower can know other things, but cannot make itself the object of its own knowledge..." And the *Brhadaranyak Upanishad* states: "You cannot see the seer of seeing, you cannot hear the hearer of hearing...you cannot know the knower of knowing."
51 *Being and Nothingness*, p297
52 *A Short History of Decay*, p25. The Dreamer does not understand how to Dream, the Dreamer just Dreams.
53 *Ecstasy*, p125

Thus 'wonder' is simply God waking up in, and as, the incomprehensible context of God's creation. Through this threshold, the being walks back to itself, for itself is its Unknowable Godself. This is why we must 'become as children', so that we may become Children of God, and then grow into God.

Now, Jiddu Krishnamurti, in his relentless manner, makes certain that we do not all become megalomaniacs, or develop 'messiah complexes', simply because we are God. He admonishes: "All your conceptual progress is based on the term 'to be'. The moment you use the word, not only verbally but with significance, you inevitably assert being as 'I am'- 'I am God', 'I am the everlasting'... The moment you live within that idea or within that feeling of being or becoming or having been, you are a slave to that word."[54]

All pride in being God ends when God realizes his or her own incomprehension.

As such, Jung comments: "...a man's attitude towards the self is the only one that has no definable aim and no visible purpose. It is easy enough to say 'self', but exactly what have we said? That remains shrouded in 'metaphysical darkness'... it is a veritable *lapis invisibilitatis*...[and] since we cannot possibly know the boundaries of something unknown to us, it follows that we are not in a position to set any bounds to the self."[55] Having said that, Jung suggests: "If [a man] possesses a grain of wisdom, he will lay down his arms and name the unknown by the more unknown, *ignotum per ignotius*- that is, by the name of God."[56]

Which is to say, to know that we are the God who does not understand, is to accept ourselves as being greater than we

<hr>

54 Talks in New Delhi, Nov 1969
55 *Dreams*, p256
56 *Memories, Dreams, Reflections*, p354

can ever imagine the grandeur of God to be. It is to elevate and yet humble ourselves in the very same moment.

Ramtha adds: "God is not a *word*. It is a feeling that lives within each of us. And the more unlimited your perception of God, the grander and more joyful that feeling...[Therefore] just as God is imageless, so be you. ...[For] the more unlimited your thinking becomes, the more unlimited your life shall become. ...How can you say 'This is what God is', when what God is now will not be the same in the next now? How do you perceive an open-ended universe? ...with a finite mind you cannot *reach* that far with description. Though the terms 'God' and 'The Father' have been used, they are only words to refer to...the unlimited isness of forever."[57]

Again, God is unknowable. We are unknowable. And if we accept not knowing ourselves, we will be God not knowing God.

"He who defines himself, can't know who he really is."
Lao Tzu

We wake up as God with absolute incredulity. And when this happens the word God is not even there for us to describe ourselves, only the unavoidable, staggering realization that ...I AM!

'I AM' is the indefinable Self, the primordial mystery. Realizing this, Sri Nisgardatta Maharaj offers: "It is enough to know what you are not. You need not know what you are. For, as long as knowledge means description in terms of what is already known, perceptual, or conceptual, there can be no such thing as self-knowledge, for what you *are* cannot be described, except as

---

57 *Ramtha*, p33,45,59,101

221

total negation. All you can say is this: 'I am not this, I am not that'. You cannot meaningfully say 'this is what I am'. What you can point out as 'this' or 'that' cannot be yourself. Surely you cannot be 'something' else. You are nothing perceivable, or imaginable."[58]

That is, 'I' is as meaningless and inaccurate as all other words. There is no such word which properly describes what the word 'I' attempts to describe. There is only the unknowable, indefinable, insurmountable mystery...'I'.

Sri Nisargadatta Maharaj continues, speaking from the 'I' of 'I's', he says: "I cannot tell what I am because words can describe only what I am not. ...I am beyond consciousness and, therefore, in consciousness I cannot say what I am. Yet, I am. The question 'Who am I' has no answer. No experience can answer it, for the self is beyond experience. ...I am free from all description and identification. Whatever you may hear, see, or think of, I am not that. I am free from being a precept, or a concept."[59]

And so, if you begin to know yourself as God, and you know God is unknowable, you will no longer know yourself, nor will you know God. And this recognition is, "...the consciousness which stupefies the Lord himself", rejoices Swamiji Shyam.

God does not understand being God, God merely experiences being God. There is no Knower, only the Great Unknown.

---

58 *I AM THAT*, p2
59 *ibid*, p136,152. This 'negationism' is reminiscent of Nagarjuna's quaternity of negations: "Neither this nor that, nor both, nor either."

"You think God knows you?
Even the world He does not know."
Sri Nisargadatta Maharaj[60]

Hence Antero Alli observes: "There is no Final Arrival or Absolute Enlightenment save honourable mention given to confessing ignorance. [For] as more functions of Intelligence are integrated into our perspective, our maps and definitions become more open-ended as the more we 'know', the more we realize in utter clarity, what remains unknown. Somethings are just not meant to be figured out. Sometimes all we can do is realize that we *are* the mystery itself and let it go at that."[61]

Similarly, Carl Jung, in one of his last writings, provides an interesting confession about his life, stating: "Nothing but unexpected things kept happening to me. ...But it was as it had to be; for all came about because I am as I am. ...I cannot form any final judgement because the phenomenon of life and the phenomenon of man are too vast. The older I have become, the less I have understood or had insight into or known about myself. ...I am incapable of determining ultimate worth or worthlessness; I have no judgement about myself and my life. There is nothing I am quite sure about. I have no definite convictions- not about anything, really. ...I exist on the foundation of something I do not know. ...When Lao-Tzu says: 'All are clear, I alone am clouded,' he is expressing what I now feel in advanced old age. Lao-tzu is the example of a man...who at the end of his life desires to return into his own being, into the eternal unknowable meaning. ...The more uncertain I have felt

---

60 *ibid*, p43. Thus "For the one who is liberated, the knowledge of mind is finished. In his knowledge the world, ego, and intellect is finished", states Swamiji Shyam. (Talks, Mar. 1999)
61 *Angel Tech*, p13

223

about myself, the more there has grown up in me a feeling of kinship with all things. In fact it seems to me as if that alienation which so long separated me from this world has become transferred into my own inner world, and has revealed to me an unexpected unfamiliarity with myself."[62]

Here Jung, who so sedulously researched and documented the almost wholly lost art of Alchemy, brings to us, in his own terms, the outcome of alchemy itself: the mergence of the microcosm into the macrocosm- the little mystery into the Great Mystery.

"...let there be no scales to weigh your unknown treasure;
And seek not the depths of your knowledge with staff or
sounding line. For self is a sea boundless and measureless."
Kahlil Gibran[63]

Recalling Rainer Maria Rilke's poetic passages in earlier chapters, we may now read some of his later poems with more clarity on the esoteric process of Alchemy, which he was so sublimely documenting.

Excerpts from his poem, *Imaginary Career*, express the idea of the progression from childhood wonder, to profane entrapment, to god-wonder. He wrote:

"At first a childhood, limitless and free

---

62 *Memories, Dreams, Reflections,* p359. Perhaps Jung would, in the end, agree with U.G. Krishnamurti, who unabashedly states: "Understanding yourself is one of the greatest jokes perpetrated on the gullible and credulous people everywhere. Not only [by] the purveyors of ancient wisdom- the holy men- but also [by] the modern scientists. The psychologists love to talk about self-knowledge, self-actualization, living from moment-to-moment, and such rot." (*Mind is a Myth*, p101)
63 *The Prophet*

of any goals. Ah sweet unconsciousness.
Then sudden terror, schoolrooms, slavery,
The plunge into temptation and deep loss.

Defiance. The child bent becomes the bender,
Inflicts on others what he once went through.
Loved, feared, rescuer, wrestler, victor,
He takes his vengeance, blow by blow.

And now in vast, cold, empty space, alone.
Yet hidden deep within the grown-up heart,
A longing for the first world, The ancient one...

Then, from His place of ambush, God leapt out."

      Rilke is poetically suggesting that at the end of all the
confusion, losses, and madness, that which was dis-*solved* (our
false self) is coagulated back into our true 'I AM', our god-self.
      This event- of God leaping out from his or her hiding
place within us- is the culmination of The Great Work of
Alchemy, which is again synopsized beautifully in one of Rilke's
last poems, *As once the winged energy of delight*:

"As once the winged energy of delight
carried you over childhood's dark abysses,
now beyond your own life build that great
arch of unimagined bridges.

Wonders happen if we can succeed
In passing through the harshest danger;
But only in a bright and purely granted
Achievement can we realize the wonder.

To work *with* Things in the indescribable

Relationship is not too hard for us;
The pattern grows more intricate and subtle,
And being swept along is not enough.

Take your practiced powers and stretch them out
Until they span the chasm between two
Contradictions... For the god wants to know himself in you."

There it is. The gross made spirit, the lead made gold, the profane made divine, the mortal immortalized, the self made Self, the little 'I' become All, the reasonable returned to mystery.

This goal- that the individual awakens to his or her mysterious godself- was acknowledged by Aleister Crowley, arguably one of the master alchemists of recent times. He offers: "Every man and woman is not only a part of God, but the Ultimate God. 'The Centre is everywhere and the circumference nowhere.' The old definition of God takes new meaning for us. Each of us is the One God. ...Each simple elemental Self is supreme, Very God of Very God... [And] man has veiled himself too long from his own glory... But Truth shall make him free. ...The Great Work is to make these veils transparent."[64]

We must slow down, be calm, remain innocent, and simply accept and enjoy our intimacy with, and as, the entire field of the Mystery of Being. After all, we are God. We must accept our mysteriousness.

---

64 *The Law is for All*, p75-81. The reader should note, however, that there are many more aspects and sublime 'steps' in the alchemical process, none of which have been described here. I do not attempt in any way to lay down even a thin foundation for the stages of the Work. Those individuals who are destined or earnest enough to pursue this path will no doubt find what they seek in other books on the great Art of Alchemy. I am here simply pointing out that, as Chuang Tzu proclaimed in a quote earlier, "The greatest art is like stupidity."

"There is no mystery about the inner life
except the mystery of godliness."
Joel Goldsmith[65]

But what then does it 'mean' to be God? What does it mean to be God's 'I', God's self, the great mystery, immanent within us? Well, perhaps it does not mean anything at all, at least not to our limited forms of understanding. Perhaps the God which is unknowable within us, which we are, should never be given any characteristics, any limitations, any definitions, or preconditions. For that is the only way in which God is not limited, and therefore the only way in which our true selves are not limited.

To accept this is to accept a powerful and troubling truth- that we must release every idea and supposition about what the self is, about what our 'I' is, and become naught but a vast and imponderable mystery to ourselves. We must cease creating definitions and descriptions for ourselves, and allow that we are so implausibly enigmatic that we are far beyond our ability to understand ourselves.

Ken Wilber relates how this possibility- of accepting our impossibility- comes about. He states: "All those things that you know about yourself are precisely not the real Self. Those are not the Seer; those are simply things that can be *seen*. All of those objects that you describe when you 'describe yourself' are actually *not* your real Self at all... The deeply inward Self is witnessing the world out there, and it is witnessing all your interior thoughts as well. This Seer sees the ego, and sees the body, and sees the natural world. All of those parade by 'in front' of this Seer. But the Seer itself cannot be seen. ...It is utterly timeless, spaceless, objectless. And therefore it is

---

65 *The Infinite Way*, p70

radically and infinitely free of the limitations and constrictions of space and time and objects- and radically free of the torture inherent in those fragments. ...Some would call it God, or Goddess, or Tao, of Brahman, or Keter, or Rigpa, or Dharmakaya, or Maat, or Li. ...Amazing! Miraculous by any other name."[66]

It is apparent that every definition, aspect, or characteristic which we had to renounce from our idea of God, as in the last chapter, must now be applied to our own most inward self, our 'I', for they are the same thing, and therefore we cannot claim to know one while not knowing the other.

If we are God, then we are limitless mystery- limitless enough to contain an infinity of limited ones.[67]

This is an old truth which we have been offered from day one; Christ admonished us two-thousand years ago, "Is it not written- Ye are Gods?" And yet we believed it not.

"It is that which you have sought to understand from the beginning of time. The Great Mystery, the Endless Enigma, the eternal truth. There is only One of Us, and so, it is THAT WHICH YOU ARE."
God[68]

Perhaps it is time we grew up and got on with the show.

---

66 *A Brief History of Everything*, p221-226
67 Thomas Carlyle wrote: "...this so solid-seeming World, after all, were but an air-image, our ME the only reality: and Nature, with its thousandfold production and destruction, but the reflex of our inward Force, the 'phantasy of our Dream'; or what the Earth-Spirit in *Faust* names it, *the living visible Garment of God.* ...[For] the mystery of a Person, indeed, is ever divine to him that has a sense for the God-like." (*Sartor Restorus*, p41,99)
68 *Conversations with God III*, by Neale Donald Walsch, p181

We are the Creators of the Creation. We are the Dreamers of the Dream. We are the Eye of the I. We have found ourselves inside what we claimed we did not know was us.

The *Gospel of Truth*, from *The Nag Hammadi Library*, relates: "The gospel of truth is a joy for those who have received from the Father of truth the grace of knowing him... For he discovered them in himself, and they discovered him in themselves, the incomprehensible, inconceivable one, the Father, the perfect one, the one who made all things."[69]

The unique mystic, Neville, provides another exegesis on the matter, suggesting: " Hear, O man made of the very substance of God: You and God are one and undivided! Man, the world, and all within it are conditioned states of the unconditioned one, God. You are this one; you are God conditioned as man. All that you believe God to be, you are; but you will never know this to be true until you stop claiming it of another, and recognize this seeming other to be yourself. God and man, spirit and matter, the formless and the formed, the creator and the creation, the cause and the effect, your Father and you are one. This one, in whom all conditioned states live and move and have their being, is your I AM, your unconditioned consciousness. ...[Such that] as the conditioned state, I (man) might forget *who* I am, or *where* I am, but I cannot forget *that* I AM."[70]

---

69 Let the reader be reminded that the 'gendering' of God, or the Source, as masculine here, is balanced by Ida Mingle who claims, "...until the establishment of the immortal plane of Being, the Mother is the Mystery" (*The Science*, p684), and by the *kun byed rgyal po'i mdo*, which is written in the voice of the Mother throughout its lengthy dissertation. Her declaration runs as follows: "Oh great bodhisattva! As to My own being, becoming evident, I teach the following with certainty: I am actuating you, which is the revelation of My own being, and which comes forth as your own being. ...Oh great bodhisattva, listen! I shall explain your own being to yourself. Your self is Me, the All-Creating. From the primordial, I am the mind of perfect purity. ...I, the All-Creating Sovereign, have become present in your own mind as the teacher. ...Because you are not second to Me, I am present in you." (p93,118,110)

70 *Resurrection*, p117,118

The acceptance that our 'I AM' is God's 'I AM' is the recognition relentlessly brought forth in the 'I AM Teachings' of St. Germain and other 'ascended' masters, published by the St. Germain press. They contend that it is only in the realization that our self is God's Self that we truly are God.

"The 'I AM' is the Fathomless Mind of God."
Saint Germain[71]

Joseph Benner conveys this point emphatically, writing from the 'I' in all of us: "I! Who am I?- I AM *You*…Yes, I AM *You*, *Your* SELF; that part of you who says I AM and *is* I AM… I, your *Divine* SELF. …You are an expression of Me, because only through You, My Attribute, can I express My Self, can I BE. I AM because You Are. You ARE because I AM expressing My SELF. …You are a human personality, yet You are Divine [; the] first of these truths you believe, the latter you do not believe. Yet *both* are true- *That* is the mystery. …[Therefore] Be still! And KNOW- I AM- GOD."[72]

So when we finally come to this outlandish observance, perhaps we will also shout in exaltation with Nijinski, "I am God, I am God, I am God."[73]

And perhaps, just like him, we will all need to fall down in ignominious wonder at the incomprehensible actuality that WE ARE THE GREAT-ONE-MYSTERY WHICH IS GOD.

"Then shall the Vision of the Lord be granted unto thee,
And seeing Him shalt thou behold

---

71 *The I AM Discourses*, p71
72 *The Impersonal Life*, p87,130,156
73 *Nijinski's Diaries*, p136

The Shining One
Who is thine own true Self..."[74]

    Therefore, we now understand our Work- to know our own divine unknowable selves; to be and to see mystery everywhere, and in everyone.[75]
    Only then will a new age dawn, division will become unified, time will end, love will fill everything...

"And the mystery of God shall come to an end."
Revelation 10:5

*****

---

74 *The Meditation on Samehk*
75 The fruit of such labors, suggests Rudolph Steiner, is this: "The greatest contribution to the development of spiritual life and culture will be accomplished when...man will meet man in such a way that one will sense the sacred mystery of the other." (*Life Between Death and Rebirth*, p78)

"Come, **amigo,** *throw away your mind."*
Malcolm Lowry

BIBLIOGRAPHY

-Alipi. *The Salt of Nature Regenerated*, quoted in Herbert Silberer's, *Hidden Symbolism of Alchemy and the Occult Arts*, p153. NY 1971
-Alli, Antero. *Angel Tech*. New Falcon Publications, CA 1991
-Appolinaire, Guillaume
-Artaud, Antonin. *Selected Writings of Artaud*. Farrar, Straus, and Giroux. 1988
-*Astavakra Gita*
-Augustine, Saint
-Bach, Richard. *The Bridge Across Forever*. William Morrow and Co. Ltd. USA. 1984
-Baha'u'llah. *Gleanings from the Writings of Baha'u'llah*. Nine Pines Publishing, 1977
      Kitab-i-lquan. Bahai Distribution Service
-Barbusse, Henri. *The Inferno*
-Barker, Elsa. *Letters from a Living Dead Man*. Mitchell Kennerley, NY. 1916
-Becker, Ernest. *The Denial of Death*. MacMillan Publishing Co, Inc. NY, 1973
-Becket, Samuel. *Malloy, Malone Dies, The Unnameable*. Alfred A. Knopf Publishing
-Benner, Joseph. *The Impersonal Life*. Sun Publishing Co. Tonowanda. 1974
-*Bhagavad-Gita*. Annie Besant translation. The Theosophical Publishing House. Madras, 1904
-Blake, William. *Collected Works*
-Blavatsky, H.P. *The Voice of Silence*. The Theosophical Publishing House, Madras, 1889
-Blue Rodeo. from the album *Five Days in July*
-Bohr, Niels. from *Beyond Einstein*, by Michio Kaku and Jennifer Thompson. Doubleday. 1995
-*Brhadaranyak Upanishad*
-Bukowski, Charles. *Burning in Water, Drowning in Flame*. Black Sparrow Press. 1983
-Bunyan, John. *Pilgrim's Progress*
-Byron, Lord. *Manfred*
-Campbell, Joseph. *Myths to Live By*. Bantam, USA 1972. Quoted in Phil Cousineau's *The Art of Pilgrimage*
      Oriental Mythology. Penguin. NY, 1962
-Carlyle, Thomas. *Sartor Restorus*. S.M. Dent and Sons Ltd. London, 1967
-Castaneda, Carlos. *The Art of Dreaming*. Harper Collins Publishers, Inc. London, 1993
      Tales of Power. Pocket Books, NY. 1974
-Chardin, Pierre Tielhard de
-Chesterton, G.K. *St. Francis of Assisi*. Image Books. USA. 1957
-Chiles, Pila. *The Secrets and Mysteries of Hawaii*. Health Communications Inc. USA, 1995
-Chirico, Georges de
-Cioran, E.M. *A Short History of Decay*. Trans. Richard Howard. The Viking Press. NY, 1975
      The Trouble With Being Born. Arcade Publishing. NY, 1998

-Clarke, Lindsay. *Chymical Wedding*. Ivy Books
-Claypool, John. *The Light Within You*. Word Book, Waco Texas. 1983
-Cleary, Thomas. *Zen Essence*. Shambhala Publications, Inc. Boston, 1989
-*Cloud of Unknowing, The*. Penguin Books. London, 1961
-Côtē, Patrick. in conversation
-Crowley, Aleister. *Book of Lies*. Samuel Weiser, USA. 1986
    Collected Works
    The Book of Thoth, Samuel Weiser, ME. 1969
    The Law is for All. New Falcon Publications, USA.
-Dante, Alighieri. *Paradiso*
-Dass, Ram.
-Daumal, Rene.
-Dement, Iris. From the album *Infamous Angel*.
-DeRohan, Ceanne. *Original Cause*. Four Winds Publications, NM. 1986
-Dillard, Annie. *Pilgrim at Tinker Creek*. HarperTrade, USA. 1998
-Dogen
-Dostoyevsky, Fyodor. *The Idiot*. Raduga Publishers. Moscow, 1971
-Dzogchen
-Eagle, Chokecherry Gall. *Beyond the Lodge of the Sun*. Element Books, MA. 1997.
-Eckhart, Meister. *Meister Eckhart*. Raymond Bernard Blakney trans. Harper and Row Publications. New York, 1941
-Einstein, Albert
-Eliot, T.S. *Ash Wednesday*
-Freud, Sigmund
-Fynn. *Mr. God, This Is Anna*. William Collings Sons and Co. Ltd. Glasgow, 1974
-Gasset, Jose Ortga Y. *The Revolt of the Masses*.
-Germain, St. *The I AM Discourses*. St. Germain Press. USA
-Gibran, Kahlil. *Gibran Love Letters*. One World Publishers, USA. 1995
    The Prophet. Random House
-Gide, Andre
-Goddard, David. *The Tower of Alchemy*. Samuel Weiser Inc. ME. 1999
-Goldsmith, Joel. *The Contemplative Life*. Citadel House.
    The Infinite Way. DeVorss and Company
    The Way of Meditation.
-Graves, Robert
-Green, Roger Lancelyn. *Letters*.
-Gregory, Saint (of Nyssa)
-Griffiths, Bede. *The Marriage of East and West*. William Collins Sons and Co. UK, 1982
-Guenon, Rene
-Haldane, J.B.S. quoted in *Dreamgates*, by Robert Moss
-Haich, Elisabeth. *Initiation*. Seed Center. CA 1960
-Hammarskjold, Dag. *Markings*. Random House
-Harvey, Andrew. *Son of Man*. Putnam Publishing Group, USA. 1999
-Hawkins, M.L.
-Henley, Don. lyrics.

-Herakleitos
-Haggard, H. Rider. *SHE*. Airmont Publishing Company
-Handelsman, Judith. *Growing Myself*. Penguin Books
-Heidegger, Martin
-*Hermetica*
-Hoban, Russell. *Pilgermann*. Picador. UK, 1984
      Riddley Walker. Picador. London, 1982
-Huxley, Aldous
-Hyatt, Christopher. *Rebels and Devils*. New Falcon Publications, USA, 1996
-Icke, David. *Lifting the Veil*. Truth Seeker Books. USA, 1998
-James, William. *The Variety of Religious Experience*. Random House
      Will to Believe. Dover Publications. NY, 1956
-Jeffers, Thomas. *Samuel Butler Revalued*. Penn State Press, USA. 1981
-Jung, Carl. *Dreams*, Princeton University Press, NJ. 1974
      Memories, Dreams, Reflections. Vintage Books Edition. USA, 1961
      Psyche and Symbol. Princeton University Press. USA, 1991
      Psychology and Alchemy. Princeton University Press, NJ. 1968
-*Kabbalah*
-Kabir. *The Bijak of Kabir*.
-Kafka, Franz. *Reflections on Sin, Suffering, and the True Way*.
-Kahn, Hazrat Inayat. *The Mysticism of Music, Sound, and Word*.
-*Kalika Purana*
-Kaszczuk, Karrie. In conversation
-Kazantzakis, Nikos. *The Last Temptation of Christ*. Bantam Books, USA.
-Keats, John
-*Kena Upanishad*
-Keen, Sam. *Apology for Wonder*. Harper and Row. USA. 1969
-Kerouac, Jack. *Dharma Bums*. Penguin Books. USA. 1976
      On the Road. Signet Books.
-*King James Bible*
-*Khandogya Upanishad*
-Khyam, Omar. *The Rubaiyat of Omar Khyam*
-Kleist, Heinrich von
-Krishnamurti, Jiddu. *Freedom from the Known*. Krishnamurti Foundation, Madras, 1969
      Krishnamurti's Journal. Krishnamurti Foundation
      Life Ahead. Krishnamurti Foundation
      Krishnamurti's Notebook. Krishnamurit Foundation Trust Ltd., London 1982
      The Path. Krishnamurti Foundation
-Krishnamurti, U.G. *Mind is a Myth*. Dinesh Publications. India, 1988
-Kuhn, Thomas. *The Structure of Scientific Revolutions*. University of Chicago Press
-*kun byed rgyal po'i mdo* (The Sovereign All-Creating Mind, The Motherly Buddha),
Trans. Eva Neumaier-Dargyay. State University of New York Press. 1992
-*Kybalion, The*. (By Three Initiates). The Yogi Publication Society. Chicago, 1912
-Larson, Stephen. *The Mythic Imagination*. Bantam Books, NY. 1990
-Laksminkara
-Lawrence. D.H. *The Apocalypse*. Penguin Books, USA.

The Later D.H. Lawrence. Alfred. A. Knopf. NY, 1959
        The Man Who Died, Alfred A. Knopf Inc. USA, 1925
-LeGuin, Ursula K. from the Whole Earth Review
-Lightman, Alan. Einstein's Dreams. Warner Books, USA. 1994
-Lima, Frank de. quoted in Hana Hou magazine, Apr/May 2000
-Lispector, Clarice. The Apple in the Dark. University of Texas Press. USA, 1986
        The Hour of the Star, New Directions Publishing Corp. NY, 1977
        Jorno do Brasil, various
        The PASSION according to G.H. University of Minnesota Press. USA, 1988
-Llewellyn, Grace. The Teenage Liberation Handbook. Element Books. 1998
-Longchenpa. Kindly Bent to Ease Us. Herbert Guenther translator.
-Lowry, Malcolm. Under the Volcano. Penguin Books, USA.
-Lucas, George. Return of the Jedi.
-Machen, Arthur. Tales of Horror and the Supernatural, Knopf.1948
-MacLennan, Hugh
-Mahadeviyaka
-Maitreya Ishwara. God's Vision-The New Dawn. avail: www.ishwara.com
-Marley, Bob. from the album Legends
-Maude, Aylmer. Life of Tolstoy.
-McKenna, Terrence and Dennis
-The Meditation on Samehk. in Paul Foster Case's The Book of Tokens. Builders of the
Adytum, 1989
-Mencken, H. L.
-Merton, Thomas. The Wisdom of the Desert. New Directions Publishing
-Miller, Henry. Black Spring. Grove Atlantic. USA, 1989
        Big Sur and the Oranges of Hieronymus Bosch. New Directions, 1978
        The Colossus of Marousi, Penguin Books Ltd. England, 1941
        The Hamlet Letters. Michael Hargraves editor. Capra Press
        Plexus. Granada Publishing. London, 1965
        a smile at the foot of the ladder. W.W. Norton. USA, 1978
        Sexus. Harper Collins Publishers. 1993
        This is Henry, Henry Miller from Brooklyn
        Tropic of Cancer. Grove Press Inc. USA, 1961
        Tropic of Capricorn. Grove Press Inc. USA, 1961
        The Wisdom of the Heart. New Directions. USA, 1941
-Millman, Dan. The Laws of Spirit. HJ Kramer Inc. CA, 1995
-Milne, A.A. Winnie the Pooh. Penguin Putnam Books
-Mingle, Ida. The Science of Love and Key to Immortality: The Third Testament. College
of Christianity. CA, 1926
        Steps in the Way. School of Liveable Christianity. Chicago, 1930
-Moore, Tom. from Images of the Untouched. Joanne Stroud and Gail Thomas editors.
Dallas Institute of Humanities and Culture. USA, 1982
-Morris, Claire. The Haven Book, from The Haven, on Gabriola Island, BC
-Morrison, Jim. lyrics
-Morrison, Van. lyrics
-Moss, Richard. The Black Butterfly. Celestial Arts Publishing Company. 1987

-Moss, Robert. *Dreamgates*. Three Rivers Press. NY. 1998
-Nagarjuna
-*Nag Hammadi Library, The* (*Allogenes, Gospel of Thomas, Gospel of Truth, Thunder Perfect Mind, Treatise on Resurrection.*) New York, 1977
-Nemerov, Howard. from *The Western Approaches*. The University of Chicago Press. 1975
-Neville. *The Law and the Promise*. DeVorss and Company. CA, 1961
    Resurrection. DeVorss and Company, CA. 1966
-Nietzsche, Friedrich. *Beyond Good and Evil*. Dover Publications, Ltd. London, 1997
    The Birth of Tragedy. Cambridge University Press
    The Joyful Wisdom
-Nijinsky, Vaslav. *The Diary of Vaslav Nijinsky*. Farrar, Straus, and Giroux.
-Nin, Anais. *Anais Nin's Diaries*. Harcourt, 1967
    The Voice
-Nisargadatta Maharaj, Sri. *I AM THAT*. Chetana Publications, Bombay, 1993
-O'Donohue, John. *Anam Cara*. Bantam. UK, 1997
-Osho (Bhagwan Sree Rajneesh). *The Book of Secrets*. Saint Martin's Press.
    Ecstasy: The Language of Existence. Diamond Pocket Books Ltd. New Delhi, 1992.
    In search of Miracles
    Kundalini. Sterling Publishers, New Delhi, 1997
    The Rebel. Hind Pocket Books Ltd. Delhi, 1996
-Oliver, Mary. *When Death Comes*. From *New and Selected Poems*. Beacon Press. USA.
-Pagels, Elaine. *The Gnostic Gospels*. Vintage Books, New York, 1979
-Palamas, Gregory. Cited in Cioran's *The Trouble With Being Born*
-Pascal, Blaise
-Pearce, Joseph Chilton. *A Crack in the Cosmic Egg*. Crown Publishing Group. USA.
-Peddie, Michael. *Where Whales Love to Boogie*
-Pink Floyd. from the album *The Wall*
-Prophet, Elizabeth Claire. *Corona Class Lessons*. Summit University Press. USA, 1986
-Proust, Marcel
-Ramakrishna, Sri. *Memoirs of Ramakrishna*. Editor, Abhedananda. Ramakrishna Vedanta Math. Calcutta, 1967
-Ramtha, *Ramtha*, edited by Steven Lee Weinberg. Sovereignty Inc. Eastsound WA, 1986
    Destination Freedom I and II, Ramtha and Douglas Mahr Prentice Hall Press, NY. 1988
-Rank, Otto. Beyond Psychology. Dover Publications. NY, 1941
-Rimbaud, Arthur
-Rilke, Rainer Maria. *You are the Future*.
    Selected Poems. Stephen Mitchel trans. Vintage International Edition. USA, 1989
-Roerich, Nicholas. *Shambhala*. Aravali Books International. New Delhi, 1997
-Rumi. *The Essential Rumi*. trans. Coleman Barks. HarperCollins. USA.
-Rush. lyrics
-Russell, Bertrand

-Sahn, Seung
-Salinger, J.D. *Seymour- An Introduction*. Little, Brown, and Company, USA
-Sartre, Jean Paul. *Being and Nothingness*. Pocket Books. NY, 1956
-*Sayings of the Desert Fathers*
-Schweitzer, Albert
-Shakespeare, William. *Hamlet*
-Shankara. *The Crest Jewel of Discrimination*
-Shaw, Idries. *The Way of the Sufi*. Penguin Books Ltd. England, 1968
-Singer, June. *Androgyny*, Anchor Books. NY, 1977
-Shyam, Swamiji. Talks published in *Knowledge Worth Learning*. Edited by Pavrita. Kulu, India.
-Silesius, Angelus
-Spare, Austen Osman. *Anathema of Zos*, from *Rebels and Devils*. New Falcon Publication
-Spezzano, Chuck. *The Enlightenment Book*. Little Brown and Company, UK. 1996
-Stack, Mike. in conversation
-Steiner, Rudolph. *Life Between Death and Rebirth*. Anthroposophical Press, NY. 1968
-Strieber, Whitley. *Communion*. Avon Books, NY. 1987
                    Transformation. William Morrow, NY. 1988
-Stulginsky, Stepan. *Cosmic Legends of the East*. Prakashan Sansthan. New Delhi, 1996
-*Sunflower Splendour*. edited by Wu-Chi Liu and Irving Y. Lo. Indiana University Press
-Suzuki, D.T. *Essays in Zen Buddhism*. Grove Press. NY, 1949
-Suzuki, Shunryu. *Zen Mind, Beginner's Mind*. Weatherhill. NY, 1970
-Tagore, Rabidrinath. *Gitanjali*. Asia Book Corporation of America
-Tao, Shen
-Tertullian
-Thoreau, Henry David
-Tolle, Eckhart. *The Power of Now*. Namaste Publishing Inc. Vancouver, 1997
-Tolstoy, Leo. *War and Peace*. Avon Books
-Traherne, Thomas. *Centuries of Meditation*
-T'san, Seng. *Prayer of the Heart*
-Tucker, Benjamin. *OF*
-Tzu, Chuang. *The Essential Chuang Tzu*
-Tzu, Lao. *Tao te Ching*. translations by Stephen Mitchel, and Chu Ta-Kao: George Allen and Unwin. UK, 1959
-van Druten, John. Introduction to Joel Goldsmith's *The Infinite Way*
-Wagner, Jane. *The Search for Signs of Intelligent Life in the Universe*. HarperCollins
-Walsch, Neale Donald. *Conversations with God*. Hay House
                       Friendship with God. Hodder and Stoughton. UK. 1999
-Ware, Kallistos
-Watts, Alan. *The Two Hands of God*. Collier Books. NY, 1969
             The Way of Liberation. Weatherhill, Inc. NY, 1983
-*Way Beyond, The*. from *The Way Out*. Sun Publishing Co. Tonowanda. NY, 1971
-White Eagle. *Jesus, Teacher and Healer*. White Eagle Publishing Trust. UK, 1985
-Whitman, Walt. *Leaves of Grass*
-Wilber, Ken. *A Brief History of Everything*. Shambhala. USA, 1996

238

-Wilde, Oscar. *De Profundis and Other Writings.* Penguin Books Ltd. England, 1954
-Wilson, Colin. *The Outsider.* J.P. Tarcher. USA, 1987
-Wilson, E.O.
-Wittgenstein, Ludwig. *Tractatus Logico Philosophicus.* Thoemmes Press.
    quoted in *Zen to Go* by Jon Winokur. Penguin Books. USA
-*Wholly Bible, The.* Hearthouse Publishing. USA
-Woodman, Marion. *The Pregnant Virgin.* InnerCity Books. Toronto, 1985
-Yeats, William Butler. *A Vision.* University of Iowa Press. USA.
 -Zukav, Gary. *The Dancing Wu-Li Masters.* Bantam Books. USA, 1994

INDEX

240

241

In, and Of : *memoirs of a mystic journey along Canada's wild west coast*
by Jack Haas   **ISBN**: 0-9731007-1-0

"...an enthralling, true-life account..." Midwest Book Review. "...an embarassment of riches... one of the best books I've ever read.." George Fisk (Cosmic Concepts Press publisher). "...a poetic and stunning piece of work.." Nancy Jackson (*Dog-Eared Book Reviews*) "... Read in awe." Benjamin Tucker (author of *Roadeye*)

Roots and Wings: *adventures of a spirit on earth*
by Jack Haas   ISBN 0-9731007-4-5

An autobiographical account of Haas' journeys in spirit, and sojourns on earth.

"...exquisitely balances poetic rapture and esoteric insight. ...a glorious illumination of our spiritual birthright." Benjamin Tucker (author of *Roadeye*)

The Dream of Being: *aphorisms, ideograms, and aislings*
by Jack Haas ISBN: 0-9731007-5-3

A unique compendium of poetic aphorisms, transformational drawings, and esoteric insights.